A Pathway to Financial Independence

—— *for Young Adults* ——

Understanding How to Manage Your Money

Drew F. Catanese

authorHOUSE®

AuthorHouse™
1663 Liberty Drive
Bloomington, IN 47403
www.authorhouse.com
Phone: 1-800-839-8640

First published by AuthorHouse 6/24/2010

ISBN: 978-1-4520-0856-1 (e)
ISBN: 978-1-4520-0854-7 (sc)
ISBN: 978-1-4520-0855-4 (hc)

Library of Congress Control Number: 2010907405

Printed in the United States of America
Bloomington, Indiana

This book is printed on acid-free paper.

The ideas and strategies in this book regarding personal finance are for educational
purposes only. Your financial situation may differ from those illustrated and commented
on herein and as such, you should consult a Certified Financial Planner or other tax or
estate planning professional to discuss your particular situation should a question arise.

This book is dedicated to my father, Ronald, who always has encouraged me to keep learning.

Contents

Introduction

Welcome to the best, the simplest, and the most practical guide to managing your finances that has ever been written.

Personal finance is one of the most fundamental and the most important subjects in life. Yet, for some reason it is rarely taught in American schools. Upon graduation from high school, college, and even business school, very few people have the skills necessary to manage their own money effectively. For many, the world of investing and personal finance is a scary topic indeed. It is filled with a daunting number of components: stocks, bonds, mutual funds, taxes, loans, debt, retirement, interest rates, credit cards — and the list goes on and on.

Unfortunately, a large percentage of the people in our country are in debt. And many more are on the brink of becoming so. Countless millions are buried in mountains of student loans and personal loans and bankruptcy notices and upended mortgages. Many more are also late paying their credit cards and have absolutely zero savings in the bank. Every year thousands upon thousands of Americans fall into the trap of taking out what are called "Pay day loans" at mind-bogglingly high interest rates because they cannot afford to put food on the table. Even the United States federal government, which employs an army of accountants and lawyers and finance PhDs, cannot balance its budget and continues to run up huge piles of debt.

Why is this? Why are so many well-educated adults unsure about how to handle their money? Why are so many doctors and lawyers and CEOs who make hundreds of thousands of dollars each year buried in credit card debt? Why do so many elderly Americans lack adequate retirement savings, forcing them to take low-paying jobs at fast food restaurants and large retail stores? And why do most young adults in the 18 to 30 year-old age group seem so completely lost about how to handle their money? Why?

The reason why this financial epidemic has struck our country is simple: most people were never taught how to handle their personal finances. This is not necessarily a problem with our school system; it goes far beyond that. It is a problem with our society and our parenting skills. If you were never given instruction about how to live within your means and save for your future, you are at a distinct disadvantage to those who were. And if you ever watch television or read the newspaper and see the opulence with which Hollywood celebrities and sports stars live, you know that our society values possessions. The problem, however, is not that a professional athlete making $10 million per year can afford to spend more than a truck driver making $20,000 per year. The problem is that a huge percentage of Americans—both professional athletes and truck drivers alike—do not know how to handle the amount of money that they have. Both frequently end up broke.

But this topic does not need to keep you awake at night and be a cause for inner turmoil. There are ways to make money and live comfortably. In evidence of this, today there are more than 1,000 billionaires worldwide.[1] Many of these people have net worth in the dozens of billions of dollars. In the United States alone, there are over 400 billionaires. And at present in the United States, there are over three million millionaires.[2]

Yet, you need not be a billionaire or even a millionaire to be doing well financially. But one thing that many of these high-net-worth individuals have in common is a solid foundation and understanding of personal finance. Simply put, they know how to manage their money.

How are we supposed to make sense of all of this? There are other financial books to help you, but many seem to be written in a completely different language that is comprehensible only to those with an advanced degree in economics.

This guide aims to be different. This guide presents information in a clear, easy-to-understand format for those without much prior financial knowledge. There are also numerous indicators to help you find the key points and suggestions in each section, as follows:

Money Goal!

The "MONEY GOAL" indicator shows an objective or best practice that you should strive to achieve.

Watch Out!

The "WATCH OUT" indicator points out something that you want to avoid doing with your finances.

Reminder!

The "REMINDER" indicator illustrates something that you should not overlook regarding your finances.

In summary, if you are a young adult and are starting out in the adult workforce, this guide can help you. If you do not have much experience with investment or retirement accounts, this guide can help you. If you want a logical yet effective text to assist you in planning your financial future in a step-by-step progression, this guide can help you. Simply, these pages will help you decipher what you need to know in order to make sure you have enough money to live on comfortably. And most importantly, this guide will help you *understand* how to manage your personal finances; after reading it, you will have the confidence to know that you are doing what you need to do in order to be monetarily responsible for yourself and for those that depend on you.

You <u>can</u> retire some day. You <u>can</u> have money to live on and enjoy life. You <u>can</u> spend time with friends and family when you want to and not be completely tied down to a job. But first, you need to get out of debt, build savings, save for retirement, and understand personal finance. The good thing is, of course, that by reading this book you are taking a positive step toward achieving this! During the course of these pages, we will refer to this as reaching *financial independence*.

If you can identify with any of the following specific reasons, this book may be for you:

- You have never really been taught how to manage your personal finances
- You do not want to spend years studying economics or accounting
- You do not understand what exactly a "stock" is
- You have credit card debt and want to know how to get out of it
- You do not know how or why to open an Individual Retirement Account (IRA)
- You want to know what 401(k) or 403(b) stand for and why having one is important
- You are not sure what percentage of your income should go toward paying for rent, food, utilities, etc.
- You think you might not have enough money saved for an emergency but want to make sure that you do
- You would like a clear process for managing your finances that concisely points out steps to take to reach financial independence

If only one or two of the above reasons apply to you or if all of them do plus some, you will find the simplicity and straightforwardness of this book desirable. It is not written like an economics textbook. Nor is it 900 pages long and a full year's worth of laborious reading. Reading about personal finance is not necessarily fun for some people; however, it is essential. This book will help you in your understanding of one of life's most important topics.

During the coming pages many financial terms are defined and explained in a simple, easy-to-understand fashion. You will learn the steps to take to get out of credit card or personal debt. You will learn how to build an emergency savings account and learn why this is important. You will learn how to invest money in the stock market in order to make your money work for you. You will learn about the power of compound interest. You will learn the reasons for buying or renting a home. And you will learn how to save and invest for retirement. But we will begin this guide with a simple question: What is financial independence? The answer to this is fundamentally important, yet incredibly simple. This will form the very first building block of your financial knowledge.

By reading this guide, you will have surpassed what the vast majority of people in our country know about money, investing, and managing their personal finances. In turn, if you can impart the knowledge you gain herein to someone else, you will have begun to help improve our society and others too can succeed financially and provide for those that count on them.

So, if you always endeavor to follow a few basic strategies as outlined in these pages, you will dramatically increase your financial literacy and ultimately gain true financial independence. You will also have peace of mind and discover a happiness that can be achieved only when you are confident that you can thrive financially and provide for those around you.

Good luck and good reading.

Drew F. Catanese

Chapter One:

What Is Financial Independence?

What is financial independence?

Financial Independence is a function of two factors:

1) The amount of money you need in income each year to maintain your chosen lifestyle
2) How much money you have saved and invested to generate that income indefinitely

Essentially, this means that:

- To be **financially independent** you no longer live paycheck to paycheck.
- To be **financially independent** you must be smart about your current investments.
- To be **financially independent** you must be smart about your future investments.
- To be **financially independent** you must do what you enjoy in life.
- To be **financially independent** you must understand how to be financially independent!

How can you become financially independent? It is something that every person can achieve if they understand how and follow some basic yet powerful steps. As you progress through this guide, always keep in mind that your ultimate goal is to be financially independent.

Remember, too, that ignorance is not bliss when it comes to your finances. Financial independence is about taking control of your own finances and not letting others—like credit card companies and banks and lenders—control it for you.

To be truly financial independent, you need to understand and implement the strategies put forth in this book. While each of the following ideas is discussed in depth during the course of this guidebook, the basic ideas remain startlingly simple:

1) Get rid of debt.
2) Live within your means.
3) Save diligently.
4) Invest smartly.
5) Retire grandly.

This is financial independence. So do not waste another minute. Time is money! Begin reading now in order to know how to put your money to work for you. You, too, can gain true financial independence.

Chapter Two:

Debt

Debt

Debt is one of the worst evils in existence. Today, millions of people in the United States have some form of debt. There is credit card debt. There is mortgage debt. There are student loans. There are personal loans. There are "pay-day" loans. And there are many, many other forms of debt. Financially speaking, all of these are terrible for you in terms of your overall monetary health.

Watch Out!

Of all the different forms of debt, credit card debt is perhaps the worst. It has destroyed the lives of millions of people. Do not let your credit card debt add it and make sure to do your best to pay it in full each and every month.

In today's world, we have the ability to swipe things on a credit card; this essentially distills down to an "I'll pay it later" mentality and leads many citizens to much financial distress. The main culprit for this is the unfortunate fact that if people do not have the money accessible today to pay for something, they likely will not have the money to pay for that thing in a few weeks either when their credit card bill is due. The symbiotic correlation of rising debt and diminishing savings continues for so many people in our country.

This chapter will discuss a few ways to help you free yourself from debt and its many damaging faces. Simply put, if you owe others money (which is the definition of *debt*) you can never be truly financially independent. This is one of the basic hindrances of financial security and independence. Thus, not owing anybody anything is one of the basic building blocks of personal financial. In a step-by-step process, here we will examine how to be free from monetary obligations to others as we pave the way for greater savings, investing, and retirement.

One other thing to note, though: This chapter on debt is relatively short. Yet it is without question one of the most important topics covered in the entire book, which is why it occupies a prominent spot here at the beginning. But the reality is that in essence, this whole book is about getting out—and staying out—of debt, in order to be free to use your money in better ways. In particular, realize that many of the strategies in the "Savings" chapter are very applicable as ways to help you free yourself from debt and could easily have been included in the "Debt" chapter as well. So keep reading, but remember to think of this whole book as one solid unit on financial independence and that only by implementing many of the strategies discussed herein can you finally become financially savvy and independent.

Credit Card Debt

For most people with outstanding debt (excluding home loans, which are discussed later in this book), credit cards are the main culprit. According to the "Experian Marketing Insight Snapshot" in March 2009, more than 85% of American households own at least one credit card. And roughly 60% of households have more than four credit cards.[3]

These statistics lead us to even more frightening realizations. The average debt in the United States is growing at an alarming and nearly unstoppable rate. Today, the average American household has over $8,000 worth of credit card debt and no clear idea how to pay it off.

Some households even have tens of thousands of dollars of credit card debt. This is a startling statistic indeed. But perhaps even worse is the fact that during the last twelve months, 15% of American adults (or nearly 34 million people) have been late making a credit card payment.[4] That means that almost one sixth of our country had trouble making a credit card payment last year. It has become an epidemic as virulent as any sickness we have ever witnessed in the United States.

Further, credit card debt is no longer just for working adults; younger and younger people are finding themselves under water when it comes to their monthly expenses, leading many to just "charge it" and postpone the payment of a bill. An astounding 84% of college students own at least one credit card while half of those students own four or more credit cards.[5] At first glance, this statistic is not overly shocking, until you include the information that only about a third of college students have a job or a regular source of income. This leads to the acknowledgement that for every college student with a job that enables him to pay his bills, there are three college students with no job yet they still have a credit card.

Because of all this, the average college graduate has nearly $20,000 in debt, with a substantial portion of this being credit card debt.[6] And astoundingly, young Americans (ages 18-29) now have the second highest rate of bankruptcy among all demographics, indicating that this generation is more likely to file bankruptcy as young adults than were young Boomers at the same age.[7]

So what should you do if you have lots of credit card debt? It is hard to justify saving for retirement or a college fund or investing in the stock market if you owe $10,000 in credit card debt with exorbitantly-high interest rates and cannot afford to buy groceries.

It is important to balance all of your bills every month and devise a plan for paying all of the things that need paying.

Money Goal!

For those people who have no debt, you should be congratulated. Move on to the "Saving" chapter! But for those with debt, especially credit card debt, read the next section about prioritizing your payments and begin the process of freeing yourself from debt and achieving financial independence.

Debt and How to Pay It

For many people, knowing what order to pay off certain debts can be a very confusing topic. Since most people have a finite amount of money coming in each month as income, until debt gets under control it can be hard to know whether you should you pay your car payment before your mortgage, or your credit card balance before your health insurance. This section helps explain a good starting point for knowing what to pay when.

Money Goal!

A "hierarchy of payments" can help you decide what gets paid when. If you follow a few simple rules for prioritizing what you pay, you can diminish harmful interest payments and more easily pave your way toward financial independence.

To illustrate this, in most circumstances you should adhere to the following order of payments:

1) Any bill you owe to the Internal Revenue Service (the IRS) must always be paid in full and on time no matter what else you must cut back on. This includes your yearly income taxes and taxes at the state or municipal level (including property taxes or car taxes). Be especially careful if you are self-employed because how you pay your taxes can get quite tricky (you might want to consult a certified tax professional to help with your specific situation). Remember that the government has the ability to garnish your wages or withdraw money from your bank account without your permission. So in short, if you owe any taxes or liens to the government, pay those first.

2) After the IRS, any debt you have with extremely high interest is next in line to be paid if you want to free yourself from debt. For many, this means their credit card debt. Strive to pay the balance in full every single month. If you cannot and already have too much debt, the key is to pay <u>more</u> than the minimum balance to avoid finance charges and the ridiculously-high interest rates that some cards charge. Make it a priority to allot $50 or $100 more than the minimum balance until it is paid off. This might take a year or two or three. But the damaging effects of high interest can ruin your credit score and your financial health. Recently-passed credit card laws now state that any payment beyond the minimum balance must be applied to the highest interest portion of the account.

Therefore, the more you pay above the minimum balance, the better off you will be.

3) After the government has been paid and you pay your credit card balance (in full if possible, <u>more</u> than the minimum if not), pay for those things that are necessary for life. This includes many of your fixed monthly payments, such as your mortgage payment, your car payment if you have one, payments for food, and your utilities payment.

4) If you are still short on money and need to prioritize, get rid of extraneous expenses that are not necessary for living but instead are actually "luxuries." This includes cable for your television, an extra phone line for your children, the high-cost plan for your cell phone that tallies thousands of minutes a month (go basic instead), or the shiny convertible that you use to cruise around the neighborhood on sunny Saturday afternoons.

5) Finally, consult the "How to save" section in the following "Saving" chapter of this guide for ways to minimize your monthly expenses and make your income stretch further.

Unfortunately, when finances are tight, 59% of people would pay their credit card bills last. A majority claim to pay their mortgage payment first and their utilities next, disregarding the exorbitant interest rates wreaking havoc on their financial health.[8] This is a bad idea. The higher the interest you are paying each month, the worse it is for you.

Therefore, although it may seem contradictory, if you do have a large amount of credit card or personal debt (this does not include your mortgage or car payments) you should always strive to get this paid off as quickly as possible. Building an emergency savings account and saving for retirement or college can come later.

Money Goal!

Whether it takes one month or four years, it is essential to free yourself from damaging interest rates and other factors that will severely reduce your credit score.

In the end, not everyone fits the same mold and we all have different budgetary needs. In your situation is particularly complex or you think you might need additional professional help, call a debt specialist or see a certified financial planner, both of whom can help you personally get on the right track and figure out a solid financial pathway to alleviate your debt.

Debt is the enemy. No good ever comes from owing others money. Develop a plan to save more, spend less, and pay bills on time. You will be glad you did.

Reminder!

Do your absolute best to free yourself from credit card debt. The sooner you do this, the sooner you will have more disposable income to put toward savings and investments that can actually *make* you money instead of dragging you down.

Action Plan

A clever investor once said "All debt is bad. Credit card debt is worse." These words could not be more accurate. If you have credit card debt, it is important to adhere to the suggestions in the preceding pages and develop a plan for paying it off, even if it takes you a few years. Never settle for having credit card debt; it has truly ruined the lives of thousands of families across the country.

After you have paid off your credit card debt, though, you can begin saving for an emergency (as outlined in the next section) and planning out your investments and retirement. This is where the fun begins!

In the meantime, prioritize who you are paying and strive to pay more than the minimum balances whenever possible. After you free yourself from the chains of debt, <u>never</u> purchase something that you cannot afford to pay for in full at the end of the month (a home is an exception – see the "To Buy or to Rent" chapter later on for more details about affording a home). If you always follow this guideline, you will always be able to live within your means and not have the heavy burden of living each day knowing that just one more expense could send you to financial ruin.

Chapter Three:

$avings

Savings

Personal saving is one of the most basic—yet most essential—aspects of personal finance. And what is very sad is that during the last two decades the average U.S. family's savings rate has been less than 1%.[9] This means that for every $100 the average U.S. family makes, they save less than $1. This puts many people in very dire straits indeed. What happens if you have no money saved and you lose your job? How will you pay your bills? How will you pay for food? How will you pay rent?

In the news recently, there has been much talk about the economic downturn. It is no secret that this recession has exposed the financial problems of millions of Americans. Some of these problems include huge amounts of credit card debt, subprime mortgages, and little retirement savings.

For example, nearly 50% of our country has less than one month's living expenses saved and almost two-thirds of Americans have less than three months' living expenses.[10] And an even greater percentage of Americans couple these meager savings with massive credit card debt and other forms of high-interest loans. If these numbers do not shock you, they should. With adequate savings, however, you can avoid many of the financial dangers that befall such a large portion of the United States.

According to financial scholar Luke Setzer, in his short yet powerful essay entitled, "Saving for Greatness," your savings "affect the way you stand, the way you walk, the tone of your voice — in short, your physical well-being and self-confidence. A man without savings is always running. He must. ... He sits nervously on life's chairs because any small emergency throws him into the hands of others." [11]

A person with little or no savings often subconsciously goes through life feeling defeated or overcome, scared of the next financial crisis or money-related problem! Having no savings, therefore, leads to credit card debt and monetary ruin. Conversely, a person with adequate savings often walks with his head held high, knowing that he can weather any storm or obstacle thrown his way.

Something that few people realize, however, is that saving has nothing to do with the amount of income you receive from your job. Many high-income individuals like doctors and lawyers have no savings to speak of, while some traditionally "blue- collar" workers live every day with a smile on their faces, confident that if something happens they have adequate savings and will not have to go into debt to get through life's setbacks.

Many financial planners and advisors recommend that all individuals have a fully-funded emergency savings fund in order to protect against life's many curveballs

Money Goal!

As a general rule, after you have paid off all credit card debt, set a goal of saving six months' worth of expenses and do not stop contributing to an emergency account until you have succeeded.

In order to learn ways in which you can start building up a six-month emergency savings account, read through the rest of this chapter. Apply the concepts and practices discussed herein, and before too long you will be well on your way toward financial independence.

Why Save for Emergencies?

Before you can be expected to just blindly start saving, it is important to understand *why* to save. The motive behind maintaining an emergency savings fund is simple: there are numerous situations that arise in life that you simply have no control over. Should these situations befall you and you need an immediate source of cash flow, it is essential that you have the money. As discussed in the preceding "Debt" section of this guide, far too many Americans do not have adequate savings and so must charge too much on their credit cards, which have incredibly high interest rates. Then, at month's end, they cannot pay the balance due. This forms a downward spiral of debt that is nearly impossible to get out of. Therefore, once all credit card debt has been paid off and you are budgeting well enough to be able to pay your bills in full every month, the top order of business is creating emergency savings. It is one of the fundamental building blocks in your overall personal finance foundation.

While it is true that if you have a retirement account you are legally allowed to withdraw money from it in an emergency; however, this is generally a bad idea.

Watch Out!

> If you take out money from a retirement account before full retirement age you are not only reducing the money that you will have when you actually do retire, but you also face early withdrawal penalties and have to pay additional taxes on the money.

Additionally, if you take money out of an investment portfolio before retirement age or before investment maturity, you are subject to bad market timing, early withdrawal penalties, and often a delay in the liquidity of the funds. Needless to say, these are not good options. Simply put, you need an emergency savings account to avoid these scenarios.

There are many examples of situations during which you will need to have a store of cash at hand. Here are a few examples of situations that may require emergency funds:

- You unexpectedly lose your job
- You become disabled and cannot work for a year
- Your company cuts back your hours to part-time
- You begin a new job in a different city and incur moving and relocation expenses
- You have an automobile accident and need a big, expensive repair or new car
- You have a major home expense (a fire, a flood, a tree falls on your roof) that is not covered by insurance
- You have a death in the family and have to pay for unexpected funeral expenses
- Your pet requires an expensive surgery
- You have medical expenses that are not fully covered by insurance for you or a member of your family
- A parent suffers a medical emergency and lands in long-term care without the means to pay for it

- A grown child must move back into your house
- Your young child becomes disabled and you must stay at home to provide full-time treatment

And the list continues for countless reasons. Imagine having nothing saved up and one of the above scenarios happens to you. How do you buy groceries to put food on the table? How do you pay for car insurance? Can you keep paying your mortgage or rent check so as not to get kicked out of your house? Regrettably, it often seems like not only one thing might befall you, but two or three simultaneously. For example, you lose your job and in the same month your young child has unexpected medical expenses not covered by insurance; then, a few days later, your car battery dies and you need to replace it.

Having money set aside in an emergency fund can help prevent the financial devastation that would occur if any of this happened; further, it also gives you the peace of mind to know that if something unfortunate does happen, you will have the financial cushioning to ride it out and not sacrifice life's necessities or rack up mountains of credit card debt.

If you are old enough to read this book, I am sure that you have had something happen to you for which you needed some fast cash, or seen situations where others have needed emergency funds. It is true that if you have insurance, it may cover some of the scenarios listed above, but there is always a chance that it will not fully cover what you will need. And if you are laid off from your job, it is possible that your health insurance or life insurance may be cut, thus leaving you and your loved ones very vulnerable to a personal calamity. You never know what could happen tomorrow.

Clearly, saving six months' of living expenses is a lot easier said than done, however. Not many of us have the extra cash to just put away $15,000 or $30,000 into a savings account and not touch it. And what's more, everyone's individual situation might differ regarding how much money they should actually put away (for more on this, see "The Cinderella Cram" later on in this chapter).

How can this be accomplished? How can you save enough? Is it even possible for someone to be able to regularly contribute to a savings account and still have money to pay for basic living expenses? In the subsequent sections, there are numerous saving strategies that can help you establish good saving habits and help you create an emergency fund. In the "Action Plan" section at the end of this chapter, there is a brief summary of what is talked about here and also a list of good places to save your money.

Reminder!

Remember that saving for an emergency should only be done after you have paid off credit card debt that is garnering high interest and hurting your financial health.

For now, though, keep reading and start to implement the simple yet powerful strategies listed in the coming pages. Before too long, you will be well on your way to having an emergency savings fund and some definite peace of mind.

Pay Yourself First

Perhaps the simplest way to increase savings (or get out of debt) is a very straightforward concept: *Pay Yourself First.* Before you pay for everything that needs paying each month, give yourself a 10% paycheck (you can call it your "Personal Rebate") from your take-home pay and deposit it into a long-term savings account as an emergency fund.

Money Goal!

Make yourself your most important creditor and investor. Pay yourself first!

It is important to pay yourself first right when you get your paycheck, because few of us have the diligence to make sure it gets done later. We are only human, after all, and thinking "I do not have enough this month so I will do double savings next month" always seems to justify impulse buying or procrastination. This strategy is based on deceiving yourself and does not work. Be faithful to this plan every month, and never forget to pay yourself first.

Perhaps an example can help illustrate this better. If you normally take home $4,000 a month after taxes are taken out, split that amount and put 10% ($400) into your emergency fund the day you get your paycheck. Often, your employer can directly deposit this amount into an account for you. Then, after the initial 10% comes out of the paycheck, deposit the remaining $3,600 into your regular checking account or wherever you keep your money. Use this $3,600 to pay all of your monthly expenses. By employing this method, $3,600 becomes the "new" take home pay. You have successfully paid yourself first.

If, during the first month you do this, you run out of money and are forced to take some of the money back out of your emergency savings account to pay for basic expenses, then you need to re-budget: go out to dinner less often, do not splurge on a new dress or cute summer outfit, and re-think buying that must-have box-office DVD. After a few months, $3,600 will feel "normal" and you will be also saving for the future as a top priority.

This is also a good strategy for paying off debt: Pay yourself first and also pay your debt first! In other words, write yourself a 10% bonus from your paycheck and simultaneously write a 10% check that you send to pay down your debt. Then, using the remainder (80%) of your take-home pay, live the month as you normally would and see how easily living on 80% of your pay can actually become.

It seems amusing that people often spend however much money they have as disposable income, whether that is $30,000 per year, $100,000 per year, or $5 million per year. For this reason, as previously mentioned, the average savings rate in the United States is now under 1%. If you always pay yourself first, however, you will find it much easier to live within your means and have money to save and invest. You will be monetarily covered should an emergency befall you or your family and you will be able to sleep peacefully at night.

The "Christmas Bonus" Factor

There is something called the "Christmas Bonus" factor that is one of the best financial practices out there to save money. It goes like this: if you receive a Christmas or year-end bonus, do not spend it! Many people consider this bonus like free cash and rush to buy a new car or surfboard or flat-screen television. A better idea, however, is to use this money to pay off credit card debt or, if you do not have any (Good job!) deposit the bonus into your emergency savings account.

Since you are accustomed to living on your salary every month without this bonus, it should not be hard to put that extra money into savings instead of frivolously spending it. This is not to say that a celebratory dinner at your favorite restaurant is out of the question: enjoying time with your friends or family is one of life's great pleasures. But spending more than 20% of a Christmas or holiday bonus on something that does not provide financial security will not provide you with peace of mind and a solid monetary situation. Years (or perhaps only weeks or months) later, you will be glad you saved or invested the money rather than imprudently spending it. Remember, too, that any other cash windfalls you receive, like a tax refund check or a performance-related or one-time bonus from work, are included in this category and should primarily be saved.

The "No Raise" Lifestyle

The "No Raise" lifestyle closely mimics the "Christmas Bonus" factor discussed in the preceding section. Every year, most Americans can expect a raise from their employer at year's end. A very good financial practice is to never spend your raise. Save or invest it instead. The reasoning behind this is that if you spend a whole year living on a certain amount, then it is obvious that you *can* live on that amount the following year too. You do not need to live on more just because you have it.

Reminder!

If you receive a raise of $2,000 at the end of the year, the best practice is to continue living on your previous salary and put this sum into your emergency savings account or invest it for your retirement.

Admittedly, as we age we develop lifestyles that require more money: we buy houses that have mortgage payments and annual upkeep, we have kids who require a seemingly endless supply of money to pay for food, clothing, and toys, and we acquire more "adult" predilections (sharing the same cheap beer you drank in college at a romantic dinner with your spouse just is not quite like a nice bottle of wine!).

If you can always strive to live on the previous year's income and try to stash away as much of your yearly raise as possible, you will reach your life financial goals far quicker.

Pay All Bills Every Month

This is a simple concept: every bill you receive you need to pay in full every month. Smart investors and savers always follow the practice of paying all bills in full every time. Do not merely pay minimum balances on your credit cards, but instead pay the whole balance every single time.

Reminder!

After you free yourself from credit card debt, the first month you get to in which you cannot pay your credit card bill in full, cut up and get rid of the card. Debt is the primary enemy of financial independence.

What if you do not have enough money coming in to pay all of your bills? What should you do if paying everything is literally not a possibility? What should you do if the only way to pay your heating bill or buy groceries is to go into debt by charging it on your credit card? The answer to this has two parts:

- First, you must substantially cut back on your expenditures. This is simple mathematics: by cutting back on how much you spend each month, you will have more money to divert toward paying all of your required bills. (In the next section is a useful list of things you can do to make your paycheck go farther and cut back on how much you spend).

- Second, you must prioritize which bills get paid when, as outlined already in the "Debt" section of this guide. The goal is that you make enough money to cover all of your expenses every month. It may take six months or a year to accomplish this, but if you cut back on your expenses and pay that difference toward your outgoing bills, you can eventually gain control of your finances and debt.

One good way to remember to pay your bills in full every month is to set up automatic payment plans. An automatic payment plan links a bank account to various fixed expenditures, which can include a cell phone bill, credit card bill, car payment, and mortgage payment.

At the end of each billing cycle, the specified amount required is automatically withdrawn from your bank account and applied toward your balance for that company, meaning you don't need to think about it. You have no bill to send, no stamp to buy, and no due date to remember.

Usually, setting up automatic payment plans is very simple to do and can be done either online at a company's or bank's website. Or, it can be done over the phone.

Typically, this service is free to use as well. So collect all of your paper bills and go through them to set up automatic payments for the monthly charges. The hassle it saves you will be well worth it. Just do not forget: *Pay Yourself First* every month before all of the automatic payments are drafted from your account.

One caveat exists for this plan, however: if you link various bills to your checking account for automatic payments, be careful to always ensure that your checking account has sufficient funds to cover the bills. If not, you will be charged over-draft and finance fees, and this is something you want to avoid because it will quickly take away any gains you do save using the automatic payment plan.

How to Save

Saving is hard to do. But listed here are a few suggestions for ways that you can make your money stretch farther each month. This is by no means a comprehensive list, but a starting point to get you thinking about ways to save money.

In particular, if you have credit card debt and are attempting to pay more on the balances every month than the minimum (which you should be!), implement some of these strategies and you will then have more money at your disposal each month.

- Go out to dinner less often
- Use coupons to buy everything you can (many vendors will give you a coupon book right in the store if you ask)
- Buy the generic or store brand at the grocery store instead of more expensive name brands
- Shop at discount stores, like Wal-mart, Target, and "dollar" stores whenever possible
- Drive your car as long as you can and do not buy a new car until your old one dies
- Find free activities to participate in instead of spending money:
    o Take a walk
    o Have a picnic lunch at a local park
    o Go for a bike ride
    o Write a letter to a family member you have not talked to in a while
- Stop getting your weekly manicures and pedicures and instead, do it yourself
- Rent a movie instead of going out to the theater
- If you have to buy a car, look at used ones instead of new ones
- Buy clothes at thrift or second-hand stores like the Goodwill and the Salvation Army
- Find out which days local museums offer discounts or free visits and visit them as an inexpensive yet culturally enriching activity
- Resist buying the latest gadget because its price will go down before not too long
- Get rid of text messaging on your phone, which often costs $10 or more each month
- Get rid of the "premium" cable channels on your television, which can cost an additional $50 a month beyond regular cable, and watch movies you already own instead

- If you want to watch television shows, check out the shows on the computer at sites like www.hulu.com, which replays popular television shows, and scrap your cable all together
- Turn off lights in rooms that you are not using to save electricity and light bulbs
- Do not go faster than posted speed limits on highways because it uses more gas (and dramatically increases the likelihood of getting an expensive speeding ticket)
- Unplug phone chargers and computers when you are not using them because they drain electricity even when off

The "Cinderella" Cram

Everyone has heard the classic story *Cinderella*. Toward the end of the tale, after Prince Charming has found the beautiful glass slipper, he goes looking for the girl who left it so he can find his true love. Cinderella's evil sisters both run up to try on the glass slipper and attempt to cram their feet into it. But alas, their feet are too big and the cramming is to no avail because it is only Cinderella's foot that truly fits the slipper and will permit both her and Prince Charming to live happily ever after.

Saving for your future can be a lot like this familiar scene. Not everyone fits the same mold and requires the same amount of money to live on. For this reason, knowing how much you need to have saved and how much you need to cut back on expenses can really help you personally determine if you are living within your means.

Numerous factors can influence how much each person should save. For example, it might depend on whether you are already debt-free or loaded down with debt on credit cards or in personal loans. It might depend on whether you have a single- or dual-income household. Or it might depend on whether your job is relatively secure or not. In the end, though, how much money you require each month hinges upon you personally and feeling secure in an emergency.

For now, though, remember the basic principles of financial independence: Even though everyone's needs are different, being free from debt and having adequate savings and investments is imperative if you hope to one day become financially independent.

Blame Thy Neighbors

In our modern society, it is hard to miss seeing the lavish luxuries and lifestyles of celebrities. We see visions of the American Dream emblazoned on billboards and on televisions every day. Materialism is omnipresent. But a far more culpable culprit for our spend-happy ways is the person that lives right next door.

Case in point: Your neighbor on one side drives a Lexus and has a perfectly-manicured yard with an in-ground swimming pool. His wife flaunts a large diamond ring on her finger and has luncheons twice a week at fancy restaurants with other stay-at-home moms. Your neighbor on the other side drives a big, shiny Land Cruiser with a ski rack and shuttles his kids to private school every morning. He hosts backyard barbeques with friends and just made partner at his prestigious law firm. Life seems good to both neighbors.

These scenes, however, mask a deep-rooted and ubiquitous problem. On the outside, everyone appears to be doing fine and living the great American Dream. The average American exudes confidence and buys name-brand clothes to make sure everyone knows that he is doing alright. Be sadly assured, however, that many are not doing alright.

Both of your wonderful neighbors, in fact, have substantial credit card debt and stay up late into the night worrying about how they will make the next payment. Your neighbor to the right has two mortgages outstanding to help pay for the house he lives in but cannot afford, while the neighbor on the other side took just out a personal loan to cover private school costs and he is talking to his wife at night about her going back to work or they might not be able to stay in their house either. Life is seem bleak, indeed, for John and Jane Doe.

The bubble that is the American Dream is ready to burst. People are living lives they cannot afford, yet have too great an ego to fix the problem. The private financial lives of many are behind closed doors for a reason!

Remember that no matter what other people have, your situation is the most important to you — NOT that of neighbors or coworkers or anyone else!

Reminder!

If you want to truly have confidence in your life and your money, do not fall into the great circle of debt that confronts so many Americans. If your neighbor buys a brand new car, he probably cannot afford it. If your neighbor always seems to have the biggest and the best of everything, he does—but he also has the biggest debt!

The point of all of this is simple: Stay out of debt and keep saving for your future. Continue putting money away into your emergency savings after you have paid off any credit card debt. Shop at thrift stores and cut coupons and follow all of the other suggestions listed in the "How to Save" section. Do what you can to cut back expenses, not create larger ones.

In the end, when you are basking in the sun at your retirement house on the beach and sitting with your loved ones on a comfortable nest egg, your neighbors will still be working and still be a part of the giant rat race that is this new "American Dream." They still drive their fancy cars, but it sure must be irritating to still be stuck in rush hour traffic on the way home from a long day at the office!

Action Plan

Saving is important. It is very important. You cannot successfully manage your personal finances unless you have adequate emergency savings as a jumping off point.

Money Goal!

Some ways that were discussed to make sure that you save enough money include paying yourself first, paying all bills in full every month, staying out of debt, and trying to live this year on last year's pay.

But where should you keep your emergency savings account? Should it be in a bank or credit union or stuffed into a drawer? These questions are perhaps more important than most people realize.

To be sure, there are numerous places that you should NOT keep your emergency money:

- Do not stash your savings under a mattress
- Do not bury it in the backyard
- Do not put your money under a rug that your 100-pound Labrador sleeps on at night
- Do not put it in a kitchen cookie jar
- Do not insert two or three bills into every book on your bookcase
- Do not put it in a "household" safe, even if it is fire-proof and reinforced with steel beams
- Do not hide your money in your underwear drawer
- And definitely DO NOT let your brother-in-law "guard" it for you next to his double-barrel shot gun

If your emergency fund is too easy to access (as in going into the other room and grabbing it) you might be too tempted to spend it. You might use it for things that are not viable emergencies.

At the same time, though, putting money into an investment that ties it up for a long period of time is also a bad idea because you will not be able to access your money should you need it.

An example of this type of longer-term investment would be a certificate of deposit (which is discussed later on in this guide in the "Investing" chapter). Certificates of Deposit can have beneficial applications, but typically they tie up your money for a set period of time, say six months or one year or five years, and you pay penalties if you need to get your principle back. These investment vehicles are not a great option for your emergency savings.

The right type of emergency savings account should be in a well-established banking institution. The best types of accounts are either a high-yield savings account or a money market account, which both are guaranteed by the federal government's FDIC program up to at least $100,000 and typically pay decent interest.

Many people today are using online banks as well for their savings needs. Online institutions such as ING Direct and HSBC Direct are Internet-accessible and have no concrete-and-mortar establishments. The benefits of this type of establishment are that these institutions have much less overhead in the form of building maintenance costs, and they can take advantage of having fewer employees and so by default have less employee compensation to pay. Therefore, online banks often pay much higher interest than standard banks.

Also, online institutions often have very low account minimums, typically only $25 or $50, and do not employ fees to do regular business. The only real drawback to online banks is that because they exist in cyberspace, you need to actually mail in any deposits you make to them and there can be a 2-3 day lag time before your money is retrievable. This is a small inconvenience, however, if you gain a much higher percentage of interest paid to your account.

Another option for your savings might be at a credit union. Credit unions are financial institutions formed by an organized group of people with a common bond. (One of the country's biggest credit unions is the Navy Federal Credit Union). Members of credit unions pool their money and other liquid assets together to provide loans and other financial services to each other. Because of this common bond between its members and the lack of shareholders and board members (like at regular banks), credit unions often pay higher interest and dividends than standard banks, and have lower loan rates and fewer service fees.

Whichever type of institution you decide to put your emergency savings into, though, simply look for the highest-interest paying account you can. These are often called "high yield" accounts and offer more advantages than traditional accounts.

Sometimes, "high yield" accounts give the account holder check-writing privileges, overdraft protection from another account at that institution, free ATM withdrawals, free checks, and even a complimentary safety deposit box if available. The drawback, of course, is that you usually have to maintain a fairly high minimum balance, often between $2,500 and $5,000. If you cannot do this at first, no worries; keep your current account. But as the account balance grows and you become able to afford the minimum of the high-yield account, move it over to that account. The extra money you will make in interest every year is definitely worth the 15–20 minutes it will take you to switch it over.

Reminder!

It is important not to simply use your regular checking account as emergency savings and "mentally" set aside part of that account for emergencies only. A completely separate account is essential.

Whichever way you decide to save your money, whether in a normal bank or an online bank or at a credit union, if you can acquire at least six months' worth of living expenses and not touch it unless it is an emergency, you will be much better off than the majority of the population.

Of course, it goes without saying that if you must tap into your emergency savings you should aim to replenish it as soon as possible with future earned income. And do not forget that as you grow older and have a family or move to a bigger house, your living expenses will also probably rise and your emergency fund must be added to. But in summary, if you can acquire an adequate amount in this account and save if for emergencies, financially you will be doing very well indeed.

Chapter Four:

Inve$ting

Investing

Investing is the best way to make your money work for you. Simply put, investing is setting aside money now in hopes of it growing into more money later. Investing is a very powerful tool and ally in your financial portfolio, and can have many different component parts. And yes, at times it can be quite a confusing topic! But investing will help you realize your financial goals, and so building a solid foundation of investment knowledge is one of the definitive parts of managing your finances.

As a good general practice, you should only begin to invest money when you have paid off your debts and successfully built a full emergency savings fund with at least six months' worth of living expenses. The reasoning behind this is that if you have debt or do not have adequate emergency savings and something happens that causes you to lose your job or incur significant unplanned expenses, your investments will have to be sold to help you "weather the storm." This can cause you to incur penalties and taxes on your withdrawals, and also make your investments subject to the potentially negative whims of the market. Therefore, make sure you have no debt and sufficient savings before you turn to investing.

While growing up as kids in school, most of us are taught that people earn money only by getting a good job and working diligently throughout our adult lives. And that is exactly what most of us do, coincidently. We strive to get good grades in school, build up our resumes, and get well-paying jobs.

There is one big problem with this scenario, however: if you want more money, you have to work more hours. There is a direct relationship between the time spent working and the money people make at their jobs. The Rat Race that is this chosen lifestyle is never-ending. The main drawback to this, though, is that there is a limit to how many hours a day people can work. And beyond this, it should go without saying that if we work more hours in order to make more money, we will by default have less leisure time to spend with friends and family and thus theoretically have less fun and enjoyment in our lives.

> People cannot create a duplicate of themselves to increase working time at their job; instead, we must invest in order to make additional income. This way, we put an extension of ourselves (our money) to work for us.

No matter what a person is currently involved in, be it mowing the lawn, sleeping, reading the newspaper, socializing with friends, or even putting in more hours for an employer, you can simultaneously be earning money elsewhere through smart investing. To put it another way, making your money work for you by successfully investing it maximizes your earning potential and supplements your income with additional money. Additional money is always a good thing!

Beyond a simple source of revenue, however, investing also is the central tool to retirement planning. There comes a time when, for whatever reason, a person stops working. Most often that time is the arbitrary age of sixty-five, the age at which the government promises Social Security checks every month. But the once-giant Social Security Trust is depleting faster than it can be filled, which means that you cannot count on it when you retire. While this concept is discussed in greater depth in the related section in the "Retirement" chapter of this guide, it goes without saying that because Social Security cannot hope to fully support most working adults of today until they die, people must save and invest for their future and their retirement on their own.

Additionally, if you want to retire earlier than age sixty-five, you must have the savings and investments to cover your annual expenses every year now and well into the future.

Reminder!

> We must all invest smartly in order to comfortably live after we are done working our "day" jobs and not have to worry about a way to make money in our golden years.

This chapter will guide you through this fundamental objective and provide you with the essential knowledge relating to investing.

Why We Invest

A person must understand <u>why</u> to invest if he or she is going to understand <u>how</u> to invest. For most people, there are three main reasons to invest extra money rather than leave it sitting in a bank:

- You can beat inflation
- You can achieve financial goals (like buying a car or paying for college) sooner
- You can retire earlier

Very simply, without money that is properly invested the above goals are much harder to attain, even in the long term. If you are going to reach your financial goals with money that does not come directly from a job, you must invest.

> Once you have solid investment knowledge and begin making real money without working, investing can be a very fun and rewarding enterprise indeed!

It is easy to understand that people attempt to invest because they want to increase their financial independence, their personal sense of monetary security, and have the ability to afford the things that they desire in life (new clothes, dinners at restaurants, vacations, etc.). However, investing is becoming more and more of a necessity in today's world. The days when everyone worked the same job for thirty years and then retired to a nice fat pension are gone. For the average person living in the United States, investing is not so much a supplemental financial tool as it is perhaps the central means to afford retirement.

Wherever you live, federal and local governments are tightening their belts. Almost without exception, the modern responsibility of planning for retirement is shifting away from the state or corporation and towards the individual. Hence, today there are few companies that continue to offer pension plans as nearly all did in the past. Couple this with declining optimism as to the longevity of Social Security, and retirement planning and investing become of paramount importance. For these central reasons, we invest.

What is "Investing"?

When people in the United States speak of *investing*, they usually refer to putting money into the stock market. Investing does not have to refer solely to the stock market, however. It is possible to invest in many different areas: real estate, local or international businesses, gold and silver, municipal or federal governments, a start-up business—either yours or someone else's—, and much more. Sometimes, people refer to all of these options as "investment vehicles" auxiliary to the stock market. This section will cover many of these investing alternatives, along with their positive and negative drawbacks.

Watch Out!

Investing is not the same as gambling. Gambling is putting money at risk by betting on an uncertain outcome with the hope that you might win money.

Gambling involves poker, slot machines, sports betting, and the like. Part of the confusion between investing and gambling, though, may come from the way some people use certain investment vehicles. For example, it could be argued that buying a stock based on a "hot tip" you heard at the water cooler at work is essentially the same thing as placing a bet at a casino at a roulette table. This is not true, as we will eventually see, because a smart investor does not invest "on a whim" or use "hot tips" that resemble gambling.

It is important to note that a smart investor does not simply throw money at any random investment he or she hears about; it is essential to perform a thorough analysis of the investment and commit money when there is a reasonable expectation of profit. By reading this guidebook, you will discover the knowledge you need to invest intelligently and you will gain the ability to ponder the viability of an investment. Of course, clearly there are still risks to investing or everyone who tried it would be rich. Knowledge of investing does not guarantee success. But it can certainly help you decide what is best for you and how to approach your quest to supplement your earned income with additional revenue from smart investments.

In the following sections, many investing concepts and strategies are explained. It is important to understand some of these basic features of sound investing and then apply them on your own. Knowledge of the ideas presented herein will put you far ahead of the average investor and in a much better position to make your money work for you!

Compound Interest

In this section there are four different charts displayed, all of which offer insight into the power of the compounded growth of money. These charts are not here to scare you and pave the way for complex financial fluff. There is none of that in this guidebook. Instead, this section is here to help you understand why beginning to invest now, while you are young, is so beneficial for your future.

An urban legend states that when Albert Einstein was asked what the most powerful force in the universe is, he replied "compound interest." Compound interest is a result of a concept commonly called the *compound growth of money*. This refers to the theory that as money is saved or invested and gains interest and dividends, it can literally add greatly to itself over time without additional principal. The following simple example is designed to give you an illustrated idea of how the compound growth of money can assist you in reaching your financial goals.

EXAMPLE: You have $500 invested that grows at a 10% rate of return per year. After the first year you will have $550:
- The original sum = $500
- 10% of $500 = $50
- The total after Year 1 = $550

After the second year of 10% growth, you will gain $55 instead of just $50:
- Year 1 total = $550
- 10% of $550 = $55
- $55 plus $550 = $605 = Year 2 total

And compound growth continues: after the third year of 10% growth, you will gain even more money than you did during the second year:
- Year 2 total = $605
- 10% of $605 = $60.50
- $60.50 plus $605 = $665.50 = Year 3 total

In just three years, without adding any more money to the account, you have increased your annual interest payment from $50 to more than $60.

Imagine if you left this money for forty years without adding any new principal and received compounded growth during that whole time. At the end of Year 40, you will receive nearly $2,060 in interest payments and have amassed more than $20,570, all without adding another dime to the account. Your interest payment grew from just $50 per year to $2,060 per year, and continues to get bigger. The compounded growth of money has given you thousands of dollars!

The final point of all of this is that the earlier you start saving and investing, the longer your money has to grow for you and the better off you can become financially. Your reward will be your money compounded each and every year over the long term.

Look over the following four tables and read their corresponding explanations to see more examples of how the compounded growth of money can help you reach your financial goals sooner.

Table 1

In the table on the next page, you can see that the difference between the compounded growth of money with varying interest rates. You can see that with just a couple additional percentage points of interest you can dramatically increase the final return of principal over time.

- After forty years, a $10,000 principal invested at 6% will grow to $97,035.
- After forty years, a $10,000 principal invested at 8% will grow to $201,153.
- After forty years, a $10,000 principal invested at 10% will grow to $411,448.

Notice first how much more money a 10% gain produces versus a 6% or 8% gain over the course of these years. Notice also the dramatic difference in gains between years 30 and 40, which is where the majority of the growth happens. The growth here is dramatic and powerful. Note also that this chart does not take into account the effects of inflation or taxes, in order to simplify the calculations.

See the table on the next page:

Table 1: Compounded growth of $10,000 (no future principal)

Year	6%	8%	10%	
1	$10,000	$10,000	$10,000	
2	$10,600	$10,800	$11,000	
3	$11,236	$11,664	$12,100	
4	$11,910	$12,597	$13,310	
5	$12,625	$13,605	$14,641	
6	$13,382	$14,693	$16,105	
7	$14,185	$15,869	$17,716	
8	$15,036	$17,138	$19,487	
9	$15,938	$18,509	$21,436	
10	$16,895	$19,990	$23,579	
11	$17,908	$21,589	$25,937	
12	$18,983	$23,316	$28,531	
13	$20,122	$25,182	$31,384	
14	$21,329	$27,196	$34,523	
15	$22,609	$29,372	$37,975	
16	$23,966	$31,722	$41,772	
17	$25,404	$34,259	$45,950	
18	$26,928	$37,000	$50,545	
19	$28,543	$39,960	$55,599	
20	$30,256	$43,157	$61,159	
21	$32,071	$46,610	$67,275	
22	$33,996	$50,338	$74,002	
23	$36,035	$54,365	$81,403	
24	$38,197	$58,715	$89,543	
25	$40,489	$63,412	$98,497	
26	$42,919	$68,485	$108,347	
27	$45,494	$73,964	$119,182	

28		$48,223		$79,881		$131,100	
29		$51,117		$86,271		$144,210	
30		$54,184		$93,173		$158,631	
31		$57,435		$100,627		$174,494	
32		$60,881		$108,677		$191,943	
33		$64,534		$117,371		$211,138	
34		$68,406		$126,760		$232,252	
35		$72,510		$136,901		$255,477	
36		$76,861		$147,853		$281,024	
37		$81,473		$159,682		$309,127	
38		$86,361		$172,456		$340,039	
39		$91,543		$186,253		$374,043	
40		**$97,035**		**$201,153**		**$411,448**	

Table 2

In the table on the next page, there are two different scenarios, entitled *Plan A* and *Plan B*.

In Plan A, a person invests $5,000 per year in an account for exactly ten years at 8% interest annually. After ten years, the investor stops adding principal and leaves that money to grow compounded for another thirty years until he retires at the end of Year 40.

In Plan B, a person skips investing for the first ten years of his adult life and instead starts at Year 11. He invests the same $5,000 per year at 8% interest annually for all thirty working years until he retires after Year 40, at the same time as the investor from Plan A.

Notice first that after ten years of investing, both plans have accumulated the same amount (Plan A in Year 10 and Plan B in Year 20).

But then notice the difference between Plans A and B at the end of the 40-year period and the dramatic effects that compounded growth can have on invested money:

- After forty years, the investor from Plan A has contributed $50,000 total over the course of ten years and at Year 40 has amassed $728,867.
- After forty years, the investor from Plan B has contributed $150,000 total over the course of thirty years and at Year 40 has amassed only $556,416. While this is still a very nice sum of money, it is nearly 25% less than the Plan A investor total.

Starting to invest early in life is essential to long-term growth. The sooner you start putting your money to work for you, the more money you will have in the future!

See the table on the next page:

Table 2: Plan A (Principal 1-10) vs. Plan B (Principal 11-40)

Year	Plan A			Plan B	
1	**$5000**	$5000		--	--
2	**$5,000**	$10,400		--	--
3	**$5,000**	$16,232		--	--
4	**$5,000**	$22,531		--	--
5	**$5,000**	$29,333		--	--
6	**$5,000**	$36,680		--	--
7	**$5,000**	$44,614		--	--
8	**$5,000**	$53,183		--	--
9	**$5,000**	$62,438		--	--
10	**$5,000**	$72,433		--	--
11	--	$78,227		**$5,000**	$5,000
12	--	$84,486		**$5,000**	$10,400
13	--	$91,244		**$5,000**	$16,232
14	--	$98,544		**$5,000**	$22,531
15	--	$106,428		**$5,000**	$29,333
16	--	$114,942		**$5,000**	$36,680
17	--	$124,137		**$5,000**	$44,614
18	--	$134,068		**$5,000**	$53,183
19	--	$144,794		**$5,000**	$62,438
20	--	$156,377		**$5,000**	$72,433
21	--	$168,887		**$5,000**	$83,227
22	--	$182,398		**$5,000**	$94,886
23	--	$196,990		**$5,000**	$107,476
24	--	$212,749		**$5,000**	$121,075
25	--	$229,769		**$5,000**	$135,761
26	--	$248,151		**$5,000**	$151,621
27	--	$268,003		**$5,000**	$168,751

28	--	$289,443	**$5,000**	$187,251
29	--	$312,598	**$5,000**	$207,231
30	--	$337,606	**$5,000**	$228,810
31	--	$364,615	**$5,000**	$252,115
32	--	$393,784	**$5,000**	$277,284
33	--	$425,287	**$5,000**	$304,466
34	--	$459,310	**$5,000**	$333,824
35	--	$496,054	**$5,000**	$365,530
36	--	$535,739	**$5,000**	$399,772
37	--	$578,598	**$5,000**	$436,754
38	--	$624,886	**$5,000**	$476,694
39	--	$674,876	**$5,000**	$519,830
40	--	$728,867	**$5,000**	$566,416

Table 3

In the table on the next page, there are again two different scenarios entitled *Plan A* and *Plan B*.

This table highlights the difference between a $5,000 annual investment at 8% growth (Plan A), and the same scenario in Plan B but with an increase of 3% to the principal every year.

- After forty years, the investor from Plan A has contributed $200,000 total. He contributed exactly $5,000 per year, even as the *real* value of his money slowly decreased over time due to inflation (which erodes away at the purchasing power of money). At the end of Year 40 he has amassed $1,295,238.
- After forty years, the investor from Plan B has contributed $377,006 total. He contributed $5,000 the first year and then increased his annual contribution by 3% a year in order to combat inflation. At the end of Year 40 he has amassed

$1,846,248, all the while contributing the same average *real* amount each year. This is about a half million dollars more than the Plan A investor has at the end of the forty years, even though Investor A only added a mere 3% per year to his contributions.

The point of this is simple: inflation can erode away at your money over time, so strive to inch up your contributions to an investment account over time that will help combat this.

Table 3: Plan A ($5000 annually) vs. Plan B ($5000+3% annually)

Year	Plan A		Plan B	
1	$5,000	$5,000	$5,000	$5,000
2	$5,000	$10,400	$5,150	$10,550
3	$5,000	$16,232	$5,305	$16,699
4	$5,000	$22,531	$5,464	$23,498
5	$5,000	$29,333	$5,628	$31,005
6	$5,000	$36,680	$5,796	$39,282
7	$5,000	$44,614	$5,970	$48,395
8	$5,000	$53,183	$6,149	$58,416
9	$5,000	$62,438	$6,334	$69,423
10	$5,000	$72,433	$6,524	$81,501
11	$5,000	$83,227	$6,720	$94,741
12	$5,000	$94,886	$6,921	$109,241
13	$5,000	$107,476	$7,129	$125,109
14	$5,000	$121,075	$7,343	$142,460
15	$5,000	$135,761	$7,563	$161,420
16	$5,000	$151,621	$7,790	$182,124
17	$5,000	$168,751	$8,024	$204,717
18	$5,000	$187,251	$8,264	$229,359
19	$5,000	$207,231	$8,512	$256,220
20	$5,000	$228,810	$8,768	$285,485

21	$5,000	$252,115	$9,031	$317,354
22	$5,000	$277,284	$9,301	$352,044
23	$5,000	$304,466	$9,581	$389,788
24	$5,000	$333,824	$9,868	$430,839
25	$5,000	$365,530	$10,164	$475,470
26	$5,000	$399,772	$10,469	$523,976
27	$5,000	$436,754	$10,783	$576,677
28	$5,000	$476,694	$11,106	$633,918
29	$5,000	$519,830	$11,440	$696,071
30	$5,000	$566,416	$11,783	$763,539
31	$5,000	$616,729	$12,136	$836,759
32	$5,000	$671,068	$12,500	$916,200
33	$5,000	$729,753	$12,875	$1,002,371
34	$5,000	$793,133	$13,262	$1,095,823
35	$5,000	$861,584	$13,660	$1,197,148
36	$5,000	$935,511	$14,069	$1,306,989
37	$5,000	$1,015,352	$14,491	$1,426,040
38	$5,000	$1,101,580	$14,926	$1,555,049
39	$5,000	$1,194,706	$15,374	$1,694,827
40	$5,000	$1,295,283	$15,835	$1,846,248
Totals:	**$200,000**	**$1,295,283**	**$377,006**	**$1,846,248**

Table 4

In the table on the next page, the S&P 500 (which is discussed later on in this chapter) is tracked beginning in 1970 and extending for forty years until the end of 2009. The "Rate" column shows the actual rate of return for the S&P over these four decades, and then tracks two different investors during that time.

Investor A invests $1,000 in 1970 and then does not add any new principal during the length of the period. His money grows at the exact rate of return of the S&P 500. After forty years, at the end of 2009, his original $1,000 will have grown to $41,567. This is a very nice long-term return.

Investor B also invests $1,000 in 1970, but continues to add an additional $1,000 each year to his account. His money also grows at the rate of return of the S&P 500, though it increases much faster because of the added principal. After forty years, at the end of 2009, his investments will have grown to $477,934. This is more than ten times what Investor A's account grew to. This is a phenomenal long-term return.

It is true that Investor A contributed only his original $1,000 to the account while Investor B contributed $40,000 in principal over the life of the account. But seeing the massive gains that a minimal contribution can provide hopefully can sway you to also do what Investor B does.

As a final note, pay attention to how varied the S&P 500 rate of return is year by year in the following table. Its worst return was in 2008, during which time it fell by 37.22%. Its best year was 1975, during which time it grew by 38.46%. On average, though, over the course of these forty years, the index grew at a rate of 11.40%. This is a great rate of return.

See the table on the next page:

Table 4: $1,000 Principal x S&P Annualized Rate of Return 12

Year #	Year	Actual Rate	No new principal	With new principal
1	1970	3.60	$1,036	$1,036
2	1971	14.54	$1,187	$2,187
3	1972	19.15	$1,414	$3,605
4	1973	-15.03	$1,201	$4,063
5	1974	-26.95	$878	$3,968
6	1975	38.46	$1,215	$6,495
7	1976	24.20	$1,509	$9,066
8	1977	-7.78	$1,392	$9,361
9	1978	6.41	$1,481	$10,961
10	1979	18.69	$1,758	$14,010
11	1980	32.76	$2,334	$19,599
12	1981	-5.33	$2,209	$19,555
13	1982	21.22	$2,678	$24,704
14	1983	23.13	$3,297	$31,418
15	1984	5.96	$3,494	$34,291
16	1985	32.24	$4,620	$46,346
17	1986	19.06	$5,501	$56,179
18	1987	5.69	$5,814	$60,376
19	1988	16.64	$6,782	$71,422
20	1989	32.00	$8,952	$95,278
21	1990	-3.42	$8,646	$93,019
22	1991	30.95	$11,321	$122,809
23	1992	7.60	$12,182	$133,142
24	1993	10.17	$13,421	$147,683
25	1994	1.19	$13,580	$150,440
26	1995	38.02	$18,744	$208,637
27	1996	23.06	$23,066	$257,749

28	1997	33.67	$30,832	$345,533
29	1998	28.73	$39,691	$445,805
30	1999	21.11	$48,069	$540,914
31	2000	-9.11	$43,690	$492,637
32	2001	-11.98	$38,456	$434,619
33	2002	-22.27	$29,892	$338,829
34	2003	28.72	$38,477	$437,141
35	2004	10.82	$42,640	$485,440
36	2005	4.79	$44,682	$509,692
37	2006	15.74	$51,715	$590,918
38	2007	5.46	$54,539	$624,182
39	2008	-37.22	$34,240	$392,861
40	2009	21.40	$41,567	$477,934
	Totals =	**11.40%**	**$41,567**	**$477,934**

Stocks

Stocks are probably the most important segment of the U.S. investing spectrum. A vast majority of those who invest do so by owning stocks, which are also called *equities*. Knowing what they are and how to use them to your advantage is a very important part of any investment portfolio and one of the strongest and most profitable tools of investing.

Stocks, in essence, represent companies. If you own shares of stock, in effect you own part of a company. As you acquire more stock from one particular company, your ownership stake of the company becomes greater. Most companies sell millions of shares of stock, so the average investor usually owns only a tiny segment of the company.

> Holding a company's stock, therefore, means that you are one of the many owners, or shareholders, of a company.

Being a shareholder of a publicly-traded company (meaning a company that sells stocks, as opposed to a company that is privately held, or one that does not offer stock for sale) certainly does not mean you have a say in the day-to-day running of the business, however. You may not, for example, walk up to the central Microsoft office headquarters and knock on Bill Gates' door to give him your ideas about how to move the company forward into the future. Instead, as a shareholder you have the right to vote in elections for the company's board of directors and occasionally have a say in certain company procedures. For ordinary shareholders, though, not taking part in direct company management is actually fine. Few of us want the additional burdens in our lives of deciding how to run multi-million dollar enterprises. Shareholders instead expect entitlement to the *profits* of the company.

Why would a company issue stock? Why would the founders or CEOs of a company want to share their profits with thousands or millions of people when they could keep profits for themselves? The reason why companies issue stock is that at some point, every company needs to raise money. To do this, companies can either borrow the money from a bank, issue bonds (discussed in the next section), or raise the money by selling stock.

Stocks can be a very powerful tool to make money. If you own a share of stock and its price increases, you make money. Conversely, if you own a share of stock and its price decreases, you lose money. And sometimes swings in the market price can be quite dramatic. What most investors hope for is a generally-upward trend in stock price over the long term that outpaces inflation and thus reflects more earnings, called *profit*.

Watch Out!

It is important to note that the price of a stock does not necessarily dictate the company's actual worth.

For example, if IBM stock is trading at $120 and Coca Cola stock is trading at $40, this does not mean that IBM is worth three times what Coca Cola is worth. Coincidently, the total market value (or total *worth*) of both companies is roughly equal. It is true that a company's stock price can be greatly influenced by company performance or business practices. But this is not always the case, as sometimes the stock market undervalues or overvalues the worth of a company. Either way, however, a company should be understood before someone invests in its stock.

In the Action Plan at the end of this chapter, there are detailed instructions about how to go about opening an investment account and buying stocks.

Bonds

Everybody in life needs money. And everybody has borrowed money at some point, whether it is from a friend, from a parent, from a credit card company, or from a bank. And just as individuals borrow money, so too do companies need to borrow money at times.

As discussed in the preceding section, a company sometimes raises money by selling stock. Or it can issue what are called *bonds*, which essentially are a certain type of loan.

But no one would ever lend money to a company or government and get nothing back. Thus, when people buy a bond, they lend money to the issuing company and are promised two different forms of re-payment:

1) The lender is first promised the original invested money back (called the *principal*) in a specified length of time, which is usually between six months and five to ten years.
2) The lender is also promised periodic interest payments (sometimes called *dividends*) as a further incentive to lend money in the form of a bond.

Therefore, an investor in bonds will receive the original money back while also receiving a small payment every month in order to make the initial investment attractive and keep pace with inflation.

Perhaps a more concrete yet simple example might better illustrate this relationship between companies, their bonds, and investors:

EXAMPLE: Western Widgets wants to raise money to fund an expansion into China. The company determines that it needs $10,000 to execute this plan. In order to attract an investor, Western Widgets decides that they will pay this investor a dividend of 5% of the original loan value every year, and then—ten years later—repay the original principal of $10,000.

You decide to be this investor in Western Widgets and so buy the company's bond. You write them a check for the full $10,000 and then every year you receive an interest payment of $500 (which is 5% of the original $10,000) from the company. After ten years, Western Widgets pays back the original $10,000 loan to you as well.

In the end, you will have received $5,000 worth of interest payments ($500 per year x 10 years) and had the original bond loan repaid to you as well.

Many people invest in bonds because it offers guaranteed income in the form of interest payments, promises you the original loan value back, and can be a safe harbor for storing money without much risk. And because companies of all sizes and governments at all levels issue bonds, there are many options when choosing a bond in which to invest.

To some investors, putting money into bonds seems like a risk-free, "no-brainer" idea. While they do not offer the high returns on your money that stocks have sometimes produced, they do seem to offer numerous advantages. But one of the fundamental investing questions remains: should you invest in stocks to capture higher gains, or invest in bonds to reduce risk? Or, should you invest in both? Read the next section for more insight into this question.

Stocks vs. Bonds

Stocks and bonds comprise the primary components of the majority of investors' portfolios. But the debate over which is "safer" or "riskier" and which is more appropriate for different people is a heated one indeed.

Many people falsely consider stocks to be the riskier investment of these two vehicles especially after a powerful *bear* (downward) market has erased a stock market's recent gains. Because of the volatility of the stock market, therefore, the value of a stock might fluctuate wildly from one year to the next, or even from one day to the next.

Many investors, then, consider bonds to be a safer investment vehicle than stocks because the interest payments and returned principle are guaranteed, whereas a stock has no such guarantee. And perhaps never has this seemed truer than during the last few years, in which the stock market saw a phenomenal gain followed by a horrific loss followed by a large gain again (and potentially another devastating loss).

Watch Out!

In the long run, bonds are not always a wise investment. Bond interest payments often only barely keep up with inflation, investors usually owe taxes on the interest payments themselves, and the original principal's buying power is vastly reduced over the life of the bond due to inflation.

To better illustrate this, see the below example that extends the previous Western Widgets model from the "Bonds" section a few pages back:

EXAMPLE: You have purchased the previously-described $10,000 bond from Western Widgets at 5% interest. As above, you will receive

$500 in interest payments every year for a decade, at which time your original loan amount is repaid.

Assuming that the economy continues its historical average rate of inflation of 3%, however, means that your actual (or *real*) dividend is actually less than $500 after the first year. In other words, what $500 could buy last year can only buy $485 dollars this year ($500 minus 3% inflation = $485).

During the final year of the bond after a decade, your $500 dividend payment will only actually be worth $380 (you will still be receiving $500, but the purchasing power will be $380 in *real*—or current—dollars).

Moreover, after ten years, when Western Widgets pays you the original $10,000 back, this sum will also have been devalued by inflation. The *real* value of the original $10,000 principal will have shrunk to only $7,600 assuming a 3% rate of inflation. In other words, what $10,000 buys today can buy just $7,600 worth of goods in ten years.

In the end, when your $10,000 bond from Western Widgets reaches maturity at Year 10, you will have received $4,376 in *real* interest payments and have an original bond principle worth $7,600 in *real* dollars (totaling $11,976 in value at Year 10). After a decade, consequently, you will have earned money, but this money will have been vastly reduced in purchasing power. You will have gained only $1,976 *real* dollars in a decade—or only about $197 per year. This is not much to write home about! This sum equals a total real return of only 1.9%, which is a rather paltry return indeed.

> As an aside, the same $10,000 invested in an index fund that tracks the S&P 500 (which is discussed later in this chapter) would have returned nearly $26,000 in *real* dollars.

By way of an additional example, let's create a scenario that has three separate portfolios. Each portfolio has different mixtures of stocks and bonds and so therefore will have different growth rates. We will assume that stocks grow at their historical average of about 10% per year and bonds pay back at their historical rate of about 4% per year. Below are the fictitious portfolios, though they are quite simplified for the sake of easy understanding (ignoring taxes and dividend payments, which are discussed later on).

- PORTFOLIO 1: You have $10,000 that is invested in 10% stocks and 90% bonds; over the long run, this portfolio would grow at about 4.6% annually.

- PORTFOLIO 2: You have $10,000 that is invested in 50% stocks and 50% bonds; over the long run, this portfolio would grow at about 7% annually.

- PORTFOLIO 3: You have $10,000 that is invested in 90% stocks and only 10% bonds; over the long run, this portfolio will grow at 9.4% annually.

In the end, Portfolio 1 has drastically reduced short-term risk due to its smaller allocation to stocks, yet has much smaller long-term gains. Portfolio 2 inherently has more short-term risk, but gives a better overall long-term return. Portfolio 3, conversely, has a very good return yet even more short-term risk. Thus, because the top investors are long-term investors, Portfolio 3 is for many the best investment.

It is true that stocks do represent an investment vehicle with more volatility than bonds. In any given year (or even every day) a stock price can swing wildly. Stocks can, in fact, literally gain and lose value every minute of every day. What a smart investor must always keep in mind, though, is that the potential for stocks to outgain bonds over the long term is very great. See the next page for a more concrete example of this concept.

Money Goal!

When investing in stocks and bonds, ask yourself if you are willing to give up a sizable percentage of return in the long term in order to cut your risk in the short term. If you desire greater long-term reward, a higher percentage of stocks are probably a better option.

Stocks for the Long Run

Jeremy Siegel, in his book *Stocks for the Long Run*, makes a good point about the heated debate relating to the ownership of stocks or bonds in an investment portfolio. After much research, Siegel deduces the following:

- Stocks have outperformed bonds in only 60% of individual years since 1802, when record keeping began (which equals 124 out of 206 years, through 2008). This means that only a bit over half of the time were the annual returns from stocks better than the annual returns from bonds.
- Stocks bested bonds in 80% of "rolling" ten-year periods during this same two-century length of time. This means that in every ten-year stretch (1802-1811, 1803-1812, 1804-1813, etc. through the last period of 1999-2008), stocks had better returns than bonds 80% of the time.
- And finally, stocks produced a higher rate of return than bonds in 100% of "rolling" thirty-year periods[13] (1802-1831, 1803-1832, 1804-1833, etc. through the last period of 1979-2008).

Therefore, the conclusion is simple: bonds are a substantially higher-risk investment than stocks in the long run (ten years and greater). As the time horizon increases, so too does the winning percentage of stocks over bonds.

The S&P 500

The Standard and Poor's (S&P) 500 is a stock market index that contains 500 stocks that are traded on the New York Stock Exchange (NYSE), out of some 8,000 stocks total. While the S&P 500 only comprises about 6% of the total *number* of companies that offer stocks, it makes up nearly 75% of the *total market value* of all of these companies. This means that the monetary value of the 500 stocks that comprise the S&P 500 represents three-quarters of the total value of the NYSE. Because of this, it is considered one of the best representations of the U.S. stock market by investors and therefore is avidly watched by many.

The historical *rate of return* of the S&P 500 Index since its inception in 1926 is about 9.8%.[14] What does this mean? It means that including the Great Depression, the big oil-induced stock market decline of 1973-4, the 1987 stock market crash, the technology bubble burst of 2000-2002, AND the recent 50% drop in the market between October 2007 and March 2009, returns for this market index have averaged nearly a 10% return per year. Essentially, money invested in the S&P 500 historically has doubled every seven years or so. This means that investing money in the S&P 500 is a great idea for many people

Reminder!

Although there has recently been a severe market downturn that significantly erased much of the market's gains from the past decade, history dictates that investors should logically expect the average 10% rate of return to persist as a long-term benchmark years into the future.

Someone investing today can logically expect the historical rate of return to continue in the coming decades, and therefore with a true long-term horizon there is much money to be made by investing in this index.

So before you try your hand at "stock picking" or invest with expensive stock brokers who had great returns over the market *last* year, consider that if you tag your money to the general stock market by way of an index fund like the S&P 500, you will substantially lessen your long-term risk while simultaneously giving yourself a reasonable expectation that your money can grow at the historical rate of return of somewhere around 10% into the future Granted, recent market downturns have lowered the rate of return over the past decade. But many investors whose time horizon remains truly long-term of more than ten years can logically expect to equal the historical average of the market like many investors have before them.

Dow Jones Industrial Average

The Dow Jones Industrial Average (DJIA) is another common stock index like the S&P 500, and is comprised of the stocks of thirty of the largest and most widely-held public U.S. companies. Some of the well-known companies in the DJIA include the following:

- Microsoft
- Home Depot
- McDonald's
- American Express
- Coca Cola
- IBM
- Chevron
- Disney
- General Electric
- Boeing.[15]

Historically, the stocks included in the DJIA—which was founded in 1896—were all industrial, or focused on heavy industry like construction, railroads, and agriculture. Today, though, General Electric is the only original stock left in the index and many of the initial companies have either gone out of business or lost the stature they once enjoyed as a prominent American enterprise. Today, the spectrum of companies represented in the DJIA is a much broader than in the past and its component companies do not really embody industry or construction as they did in the past.

Sometimes, stocks are removed from the index and others are added in order to reflect a true representation of the U.S. economy. For example, the bankrupt insurance giant AIG was removed from the index in September of 2008 and replaced by Kraft Foods.

Watch Out!

The Dow Jones Industrial Average, which is often referred to as simply "the Dow," is perhaps the most widely quoted market index on the news in the United States. The problem with this, however, is that it includes only thirty stocks and therefore is not a very accurate representation of the full market's performance.

The S&P 500, as discussed in the preceding section, is thought of by many investors as a much better reflection of the overall U.S. stock market's performance and make-up because it represents a much larger segment of the companies traded on the New York Stock Exchange. There are still other market indexes out there, such as the Russell 2000 and the Wiltshire 5000, but the S&P 500 remains the most watched index in the United States because it is such a solid representation of the overall stock market.

Money Managers and Stock Brokers

There are many honest, hard-working, winning money managers and stock brokers out there. Many people, though, are confused on what each does, exactly.

Money managers manage hedge funds, investment accounts, or mutual funds, often for affluent clients or large firms. Stock brokers, alternatively, recommend stocks, mutual funds, or other investment vehicles to put money into for both individuals and firms of all sizes.

Both types of these professionals can make their clients lots of money every year and always act with their client's best interest at hand. They can be counted upon to produce solid returns on investments (sometimes much greater than the overall market's returns) and they also understand each investor's needs and concerns.

Watch Out!

Despite the brilliant marketing campaigns of numerous stock brokers and money managers, there are some in the profession who are nothing more than salesmen seeking to maximize their own profit. Be careful when you pick one!

Of course, in no way is this book trying to give stock brokers, money managers, economists, and investment specialists a bad name. As already mentioned, there are many good ones out there who always work in their client's best interest and consistently make money year in and year out.

But many people assume that if an investment firm employs hundreds or thousands of people, all of whom are Harvard MBA graduates, and it also maintains a multi-million dollar yearly budget, then the firm must employ good money managers and stock brokers for individuals like you and me. Further, because these companies have people who scrutinize Wall Street price-to-earnings ratios, every business' prospectus, and seem to know everything there is to know about investing, money managers and stock brokers would clearly make good financial decisions that are much better than the average Joe's financial decisions.

The reality is that this is not always true! In fact, historically only about one out of four professional money managers equal or exceed the market's average return on a consistent and long-term basis of ten years or more. This means that, 75% of those highly-paid, professionally-trained specialists who manage hedge funds and mutual funds and recommend all of the "best" stocks out there, do not equal the overall market's performance in the long term.

And what's more, after many of these stock brokers and money managers do not beat the market like we expect them to, they still receive a commission just for handling your money. Imagine: you pay a stock broker a commission even if he loses money! The point, then, is that over the long run there are very few stock brokers who can consistently beat the returns of the S&P 500 or the Dow.

> There is a well-known expression around Wall Street that reads: "A stock broker's guess as to the Market's direction is similar to a fisherman's guess as to how many fish he will catch while still on the way to the lake." Or more simply, *Economists exist to make weathermen look good.*

For many investors, therefore, instead of giving a large portion of your money to a stock broker to trade for you and *attempt* to beat the performance of the overall stock market, go online to one of the low-cost brokerage houses (like Vanguard, Fidelity, or TD Ameritrade) and tie your money to an index fund there as an alternative. All of these have websites that detail how to open an account and invest with them, and also all offer phone support for those people who would rather talk to an actual person. For specific strategies, see the "Action Plan" at the end of the chapter.

One additional note: there are many people who have individual financial situations that are more complex and require more explanation and guidance than a few pages could explain. Perhaps there are tax circumstances that might influence where you put your money. Or perhaps you inherited a large sum of money from a deceased relative and face withdrawal penalties or a unique investment situation. If you do not understand or do not feel comfortable with investing your money without professional help, ask around to find an experienced money manager or stock broker who charges hourly rates (instead of working on commission) and share your financial situation with him or her.

Mutual Funds

Mutual funds, in basic terms, are funds that pool the money of many investors and invest it according to their own money managers' ideas and predictions. This type of fund has become very popular in the past ten years or so because it draws upon the collective knowledge of experienced money managers and uses this knowledge to invest for average people who might not have the knowledge or desire to invest on their own.

Further, mutual funds have a large principal to invest because they combine the money from many people and so garner greater attention than individual investors might. Because many people with "regular" jobs often feel that they do not know the ins and outs of the stock market as well as someone who studies it constantly, people often assume that by investing in a mutual fund their money will be managed better than if they did it themselves.

See the simple example below that illustrates how a mutual fund works.

EXAMPLE:
Sam has $10,000.
Maria has $10,000.
Gerard has $10,000.
Isabel has $10,000.

All four investors put their money in Mutual Fund A for a small fee (many mutual funds charge a fee, called a *load*, of usually between 1%

and 5% of the total amount invested). The money manager at Mutual Fund A, therefore, has $40,000 to invest as he sees fit. Using a team of economists and researchers, the money manager determines that stock X, stock Y, and stock Z are all good investments with great potential. So are bond E and bond F. So the mutual fund takes the $40,000 and invests it all in these places, hoping that the research is correct and the investors will make money.

Sam, Maria, Gerard, and Isabel, meanwhile, rest assured knowing that a whole team of professionals is directing their money far better than an average person with limited investment knowledge could.

Mutual funds, therefore, are a fabulous idea *in theory*. Professional money managers with vast market knowledge and experience pick stocks and bonds and other investment vehicles in which to invest after doing lots of research, and these money managers do all of this for the average person who cannot devote twelve hours a day to investment strategy.

Watch Out!

A problem with mutual funds is that the rate of return of many mutual funds often does not equal the simple rate of return of the general stock market. AND you often must pay a fee, or load, to invest with the fund. This fee does not guarantee future performance, though.

The money managers hired to pick investments for mutual funds, therefore, can do lots of research on their picks but in the end, they rely on luck just like any other investor. Yes, they are very knowledgeable and read all the latest research. But just because a stock performed well last year does not mean that it will this year. For example, just because a professional football team wins the Super Bowl in 2008 does not mean that they will win again in 2009 or 2010 or any other time in the future. They might, but then again they might not. The past is not necessarily a good indication of future performance when it comes to stock picks or Super Bowl winners.

There *are* winning mutual funds out there that beat the market and make their investors lots of money. Many, however, do not accomplish this. And the only way to gauge their success, of course, is retrospectively.

In short, however, mutual funds are a great idea and many people invest in them because they feel comfortable knowing that a team of money managers is investing their money for them. But in the long run, very few mutual funds achieve the historical 10% average rate of return that the overall stock market has achieved during its history.

Reminder!

If there is a mutual fund that you think can produce excellent results in the long run, perhaps it is a good investment. But remember that linking your invested money to an index fund is guaranteed to equal the return of the overall market. There is not a mutual fund in the country that offers this same guarantee.

ETFs vs. Mutual Funds

Exchange Traded Funds, also called ETFs, are another common (and recently-invented) investment vehicle. Essentially, ETFs are like mutual funds in how they function. When an investor puts his money into an ETF, it can track an index, such as the S&P 500 or the Dow Jones Industrial Average. Or, an ETF can be actively-managed by a money manager like a mutual fund is, investing in stocks and bonds at the discretion of the money manager. ETFs are attractive to many investors because of their low cost, their tax efficiency, and their stock-like trading features.

ETFs combine the benefits of a mutual fund, which is overseen by a professional money manager, with the versatility of exact-time trading. This means that while mutual funds can only be bought or sold at each day's closing price, ETFs trade throughout the day at prices that can be locked in by any "buy" or "sell" order at a precise moment. Therefore, many amateur investors begin buying and selling ETFs as a way into the world of active trading in stocks. There is a small fee to buy or sell an ETF, like there is to buy or sell any stock or mutual fund, but this fee is usually minimal, especially at a low-cost brokerage house like Vanguard or Fidelity.

According to many investors, then, ETFs are a better choice than mutual funds because of their efficiency, their low cost, and their exact-time trading ease. ETFs are highly recommended as an investment vehicle, especially those that track an index fund and incur minimal expenses and so are virtually guaranteed to equal the results of the general market. As always, though, make sure you understand what an ETF invests in or tracks before you put your money into it.

Real Estate (and REITs)

For decades, investing in real estate has been a popular and potentially very lucrative investment vehicle. Although the last few years have witnessed a dramatic downturn in the real estate market, there is still much money to be made for an adventurous and well-informed investor. There are basically two ways to invest in real estate: direct investing and Real Estate Investment Trusts (REITs). Both offer advantages and disadvantages for an investor.

Direct investing in real estate is about more than buying a home to live in; it involves the purchase of a property with the intent of renting it out to a tenant or selling it for more money than it was originally purchased for. When a person buys a home or apartment building and rents it out to someone, typically the owner (also called the landlord) pays the mortgage and all property fees directly and then seeks to receive rent every month to recover these expenses.

A landlord can also charge more in rent than the total mortgage and fees in an attempt to make a monthly profit and have a positive income stream. Furthermore, a rented-out property may have gone up in value, or *appreciated*, and so the landlord is left with a more valuable asset than when it was originally purchased, plus is receiving money every month in the form of rent payments. The landlord can then sell the property and make more money than he might have by just collecting rent.

But as always, there are some drawbacks to purchasing a property with the intent of renting it out:

- You could have a tenant who damages the property or destroys something at your expense

- You might not be able to find a reliable tenant and thus have no rent check to help recoup the monthly mortgage costs
- The roof might cave in and you will be forced to fix it during a rain storm at 2:00am
- The property or area might go down in value and you can only sell the property for less than you originally paid
- Plus, there are about 10,000 small problems and more than a few major ones that are associated with home ownership

Some people also purchase real estate not with the intent of renting it out, but instead merely to fix up the property and sell it quickly for more than the original cost.

This type of real estate investing can be very lucrative in the right market and with property in the right places. But, like renting out a property for years and then trying to sell it, there is also a chance that the value of the house or property will go down and you will end up losing money. Thus, although direct investing in real estate offers many potentially profitable opportunities, buying and selling properties is quite complicated and requires a large store of up-front capital. There are also serious tax issues to consider. And the returns, though perhaps large, can also turn negative quite quickly. In the end, therefore, before anyone invests directly in real estate by buying and selling property for investment purposes only, they should talk to a certified estate planning professional or real estate tax specialist.

Investing in a **Real Estate Investment Trust**, conversely, offers many of the same investment benefits as direct investing with much less hassle. And the opportunity for a very solid *dividend yield* (meaning how much the investor is paid in dividends every month or quarter by the company that controls the REIT) is often higher as well.

In essence, when you purchase a REIT you are not buying a property directly but instead are purchasing a professionally-managed fund that invests in varying aspects of commercial real estate.

Reminder!

REITs can invest in many different segments of the overall market. For example, a REIT might invest in hotels, shopping malls, apartment complexes, undeveloped land, or commercial office buildings.

Some REITs choose to invest in one particular category of those mentioned above, while others invest in many different categories to diversify their holdings. Some even will invest in a particular geographical region, such as Napa Valley or South Boston. Either way, an investor buys a REIT like any stock fund and can make or lose money depending on if the REIT gains or loses value. Generally speaking, unless you are exceptionally well-versed in the particulars and idiosyncrasies of investing directly in real estate properties, it is wise to instead try your hand at investing in REITs if you have a great desire to invest in the real estate market.

A few well-known and reputable REITs are LTC Properties, which invests in hospitals and medical drug companies and manufacturers; Equity Residential, which invests in apartments and residential properties; Federal Realty Investment Trust, which invests in shopping centers and malls; and American Capital Agency Corporation, which invests in residential mortgages.

The best way to decide upon a REIT is to think of an area that you would enjoy investing in, such as home properties, shopping malls, or hospitals and nursing homes, and search out some REITs that invest in those areas and pay dividend yields of between 8% and 12%.

Also, read up about the company before you invest in it, because financial knowledge about an investment is imperative before you lend out your money. Read about things like management style, company philosophy, company history, and investment strategy. These will give you important knowledge regarding what the company is about and how its future looks.

Keep in mind, though, that investing in real estate in order to make money is not the same thing as buying a home to live in, which is discussed in a later chapter.

Reminder!

When you purchase a property with the intent of living in it, you build valuable equity while providing yourself and your family with something necessary for life: shelter. There are also tax incentives to purchasing a home in which to live. In short, buying a home to live in is vastly different from *investing* in real estate as a profit venture.

But if you do want to invest in real estate directly or through a REIT, do your homework and read up about it thoroughly while considering all of the risks involved. And remember that it is a good idea to speak with a certified tax professional before a major asset is purchased, whether for investment or residential purposes.

Gold and Silver

Since essentially the dawn of civilized humanity, people have valued pretty things. Perhaps foremost among these in many cultures have been the precious metals gold and silver, two of our earth's most beautiful substances with great inherent value. As different empires and currencies have come and gone, humans have always placed great value in these metals and, with all likelihood, will continue to do so for many millennia.

Purchasing gold and silver, or purchasing funds that invest in gold or silver, is a very common modern investment strategy as well. But it can also be a financial safeguard for many people and part of a solid life plan. Having a supply of a precious metal in your possession helps hedge against inflationary powers and the rise and fall of the value of a dollar or stock.

There are three main ways to invest in gold or silver (or any other precious metal, like platinum, copper, nickel, etc.). The first and perhaps easiest way to purchase any metal is to buy a stock fund or an ETF that replicates the price of each metal and trades like a stock.

> EXAMPLE: Gold currently trades at $800 an ounce and you buy a stock fund that invests in it. If the price of gold goes up to $1,000 an ounce, you will have made a nice profit of 25%. But like any stock or mutual fund, the prices can fall as well: if you buy a fund that invests in gold at $800 an ounce and the price falls to $600 an ounce, you will have lost 25%.

Many people correctly think that having some shares of a gold or silver stock fund or ETF adds stability and diversity to an investment portfolio. It does this because often when the overall stock market declines, precious metals increase in value. Thus, this can be a hedge against these market gyrations and provide valuable peace of mind.

A second way to invest in gold or silver is to purchase it directly. There are many websites online to buy precious metals directly and have them shipped to your house. For example, at www.monex.com and www. goldprice.org, you can purchase gold or silver in both bullion form (the fancy term for actual bars of the metal) and as coins from the United States Mint.

Many people buy gold or silver or other precious metals as a safeguard of personal financial freedom.

Money Goal!

If the monetary system as we know it were to ever collapse, having a supply of gold or silver coins or bullion can give you a powerful tool for barter; there will always be a way to trade them for goods or services like food and shelter.

Clearly, very few people actually believe that we will experience a true financial Armageddon any time soon as the global monetary system collapses. But if you want to buy precious metals to not only hedge against stock market fluctuations but also to counter a future financial catastrophe, then perhaps they are worth buying.

Numerous financial experts contend that purchasing either 1-ounce gold coins or a bag of pre-1965 silver dimes (when they were made of 100% silver) are perhaps the two best options if you would like to keep gold and silver. Some people buy these and bury them in their backyard; others put them in a safety deposit box. At $900 an ounce, a roll of fifty 1-ounce gold Liberty dollars from the United States Mint have a value of about $45,000.

In the end, therefore, owning a precious metal either directly or through a stock fund or an ETF is a very common strategy to diversify any investment portfolio. Some financial experts recommend that people keep roughly 3-5% of a portfolio as gold or silver, often as a set of actual coins or bullion that will not lose their real or their monetary value.

Non-Financial Investment Vehicles

Some people grow tired of the traditional investment options like stocks, bonds, and real estate and instead look to diversify their portfolio with alternative investment vehicles. Some of these alternatives include artwork, cars, jewelry, wine, antiques, and first edition books or records.

Watch Out!

While there is no doubt that collecting fine wines or owning antique cars is quite a bit more fun than owning a stock, there are numerous problems with this type of "alternative" investment vehicle.

First, many of these non-financial investments need to be insured. For example, you would not own a $20,000 diamond ring or a 1908 Ford Model T without purchasing insurance to protect these investments. But buying insurance on an investment erodes at any appreciation of the value it might gain while you own it. Simply, you have to *pay* to own one of these investment types. This makes no financial sense.

Second, and perhaps more importantly, there is no guarantee that any of the abovementioned objects will ever appreciate in value (though the same could be argued for any investment, of course). To more clearly illustrate this point, consider the following situation:

Diego Velazquez, Spain's most famous artist of the Baroque Period, painted the bulk of his work in the mid-1600s. Today, many of his masterful paintings can be seen in the renowned Prado Museum in Madrid, including his best-known work *Las Meninas*. Right after it was painted in 1656, *Las Meninas* reputedly sold for around $100. Today, the painting's worth is estimated at about $100 million.

Does this seem like a solid investment? It does until you break down the finances behind it. We know that the painting sold for $100 in 1656 and grew in value to approximately $100 million today. But this represents an annualized growth rate of only just over 3%, which is about the same rate as the historical U.S. average of inflation.

Thus, as an investment *Las Meninas* grew at a sluggish 3% growth rate; or, more simply, this means that the painting actually did not grow in *real* value over the last 350 years when inflation averages are taken into account. Essentially, $100 in 1656 equals about $100 million in current dollars.

This example illustrates that many things which seem like "a good store of value" are, in fact, terrible financial investments for those seeking to make a profit. These types of investments, then, have value that exists for sentimental or pleasurable reasons but not for money making reasons. Own them and enjoy them, but do not rely on them to produce sustained income that you need in order to survive.

And further, very few people can afford to just plop down $20,000 for a diamond ring or $80,000 for an antique car as an investment (or $100 million for a painting!). For many, this is not a possibility.

But consider this last twist to the preceding example: Let's say that instead of purchasing *Las Meninas* in 1656, the purchaser invests the same $100 in a stock market index fund that garners an 8% return (there was no stock market back then, but we'll assume there was one for the sake of this example). After these 350 years, the original $100 would be worth over $46 trillion dollars today, following the average growth rates of the stock market. With this sum, you could pay off the U.S. National Debt nearly four times over. Now that is a good return on investment!

Annuities

Annuities are products sold by insurance companies or special divisions of financial institutions that are designed to provide guaranteed income for an investor over an extended period of time. Typically, annuities are purchased by older people as a source of guaranteed retirement income.

There are basically two types of annuities: tax-deferred annuities and immediate annuities, both of which are explained in detail in the coming pages.

TYPE ONE: Tax-Deferred Annuities

Tax-deferred annuities come in two forms: fixed-rate and variable-rate. Because the U.S. government allows cash deposited in insurance contracts to grow tax-deferred (meaning all earnings grow tax-free until money is taken out), think of these annuities almost like a create-your-own pension system. The two different types of tax-deferred annuities are explained below.

- **Fixed-rate annuities**
  When you invest in a fixed-rate annuity, you contribute money either in a lump sum or in regular installments over a predetermined number of years and the money grows at a fixed minimum rate. When the annuity reaches maturity, typically at retirement age, the insurance company will pay you a fixed dollar amount for the life of the annuity or until your death.

- **Variable-rate annuities**
  When you invest in a variable-rate annuity, you contribute money like you would to a fixed-rate annuity, either as a lump sum or in regular installments. But with variable-rate annuities you have the freedom to invest in mutual funds that can potentially offer more room for earnings growth. At an agreed-upon date, again typically retirement age, the insurance company will begin making payments based on the value of your annuity. Basically, if the annuity value grows due to stock market gains, you will receive a larger income payout; conversely, if the annuity value decreases due to stock market losses, you will receive a smaller income payout.

TYPE TWO: Immediate Annuities

Immediate annuities are the other popular choice for those wishing to invest in a fixed source of income. With this type of annuity, an investor pays a lump sum directly to an insurance company and from that point forward receives regular payments based on the size of the original lump sum for a specified number of years or until death.

EXAMPLE: You buy a $300,000 immediate fixed-rate annuity paying 5% interest, and from that point forward you will receive $15,000 (5% of $300,000) every year for the remainder of your life. The amount received will never go up or down, but instead remains constant.

Most people who buy immediate annuities are people at retirement age who desire a guaranteed source of income for the rest of their lives, much like a pension. Because they typically require a big up-font payment in cash and tie up this money forever, only retirees should normally buy an immediate annuity.

Beyond straight-forward tax-deferred and immediate annuities, there are numerous options and alternatives to buy as well, which become a bit more complicated.

Some of these more complex options include:

- Inflation-linked annuities whose payouts increase at the rate of inflation every year
- Double-life annuities whose payouts benefit the spouse or another designated beneficiary should the original investor die before the full maturity date of the annuity
- Refund-of-Premium annuities whose payments over the years get returned minus any gains or earnings upon the death of the investor
- Deferred variable annuities with guaranteed minimum withdrawal or income benefits

If you wish to purchase one of the above mentioned annuities, it is probably best to consult a certified financial planner or estate specialist because there are many regulations governing how they function.

Reminder!

In the end, many older people purchase an annuity to provide a guaranteed source of income in the future. For more information, consult the following websites:

- http://www.sec.gov/investor/pubs/varannty.htm
- http://www.freeannuityrates.com

Certificates of Deposit

Certificates of Deposit (CDs) are essentially deposits to a financial institution for a set length of time. In this way, they are actually similar to an annuity. When you purchase a Certificate of Deposit, you invest a fixed sum of money for a fixed period of time—anywhere from three months to five years or more—and, in exchange, the issuing bank pays you interest at a set rate, typically at regular intervals throughout the life of the CD. When you cash in or redeem your CD, you receive the money you originally invested plus you receive any accrued interest that the deposited money might have earned over the length of the CD. Certificates of Deposit, then, are also in some ways similar to a bond, which was discussed earlier in this book. CDs are usually insured by the Federal Deposit Insurance Corporation (FDIC) and thus they are virtually risk-free stores of money.

Watch Out!

Some people think of CDs as an alternative to a savings account, but this is incorrect thinking. CDs are designed to be held until maturity, and so are less accessible than money in a savings account at a bank that can be accessed at any time.

Withdrawals from a CD before maturity are usually subject to a substantial penalty. For a five-year CD, this penalty is often the loss of six months' worth of interest. These penalties ensure that it is generally in the holder's best interest not to withdraw the money from the CD until it reaches maturity. Therefore, only purchase a CD if you do not plan to need this money until the CD has matured.

EXAMPLE: You buy a $10,000 one-year CD from your bank that pays 5% interest.
- Every month you receive about $42 in interest payments:
    o   5% of $10,000 = $500 per year
    o $500 divided by 12 months = $42
- After the one-year maturity, the original $10,000 is repaid to you along with any interest that the principal has gained itself over the CD duration.

Many people hold CDs as part of their investment portfolio because they often garner slightly greater interest rates than a regular savings account does.

Money Goal!

If you do decide to purchase a CD as part of your investment portfolio, however, make sure that you already have six months' worth of living expenses in a savings account that you can access at any time in case of an emergency.

For most people, buying a CD is a viable option only if you do not need that money during the length of the CD and no other options are available to you. For most people, though, if you have additional cash to invest after you have paid off your credit card debt and funded your emergency savings account, you should try investment vehicles that can produce a greater return on investment.

Dollar Cost Averaging

Dollar Cost Averaging is more of a strategy than it is an investment vehicle. It is a powerful investing technique intended to reduce exposure to the risk associated with making a single large purchase of stocks.

The idea is simple: apply a fixed dollar amount at regular intervals, typically monthly or quarterly, on a particular investment or portfolio, regardless of the share price. It is a phenomenal way to combat the omnipresent market gyrations of the stock market and thus diminish risk. Most defined contribution retirement benefit plans like a 401(k) inherently use Dollar Cost Averaging as the primary investment strategy, to the advantage of the recipient. They do this because typically employees fund a retirement account each pay period through deductions from their paycheck. Therefore, money is contributed every week or month, which is Dollar Cost Averaging.

EXAMPLE: You put $100 into a retirement account every month, buying $100 worth of stocks.

- In Month 1 the stock trades at $5 per share
  - o $100 / $5 per share = 20 shares
- In Month 2 the stock rises to $10 per share
  - o $100 / $10 per share = 10 shares
- In Month 3 the price falls back to $5 per share
  - o $100 / $5 per share = 20 shares

This cycle of purchasing the stock at regular intervals—but not regular prices—is an example of Dollar Cost Averaging.

After these three months, then, you will have purchased fifty shares total (20 + 10 + 20 = 50). You have also spent a total of $300 ($100 per month x 3). This means that you have averaged $6 per share over the course of these three months ($300 / 50 shares = $6 per share).

At a purchase price of $6 per share, you have done well. The average price of the stock over the course of these three months was actually $6.66, which is more than you paid for it on average. Thus, your overall number of purchased shares is higher than it would have been had you only purchased the $100 worth of stock when the price was low, at $5 per share.

Of course, an investor actually has no way to determine when the share price of a stock will be high or low, something that can only determined in hindsight. Since you cannot know if today's price is lower than it will be in a month, by buying stock in set intervals through dollar cost averaging you will automatically purchase more shares when prices are low and fewer shares are bought when prices are high.

In summary, Dollar Cost Averaging's main objective is to lower the total cost per share over time, thus lessening the risk of investing a large amount of money into the market at a time when share price might be higher than desired. Dollar Cost Averaging is indeed a sound investment practice for many investors.

Asset Allocation

To many investors, asset allocation is one of the most important aspects of a portfolio. Asset allocation refers to how an investor divides or distributes his or her investments among various classes of investment vehicles like stocks, bonds, real estate, cash, or gold.

Simply, this means that if you have $10,000 to invest, what percentage of this money should be invested in stocks and what percentage should be saved in cash or gold commodities or any other investment you choose? Asset allocation as a strategy, therefore, seeks to optimize the return you receive on your money while minimizing the risk inherent in investing.

> It is said that since you cannot time or predict the market's movements, asset allocation should be the major focus of your investment strategy because it is the only factor affecting risk and return that you control.

Inherent in asset allocation is the idea that predicting the future rate of return of certain asset classes is impossible. The best-performing asset will vary from year to year, as will the worst-performing asset.

> Different asset classes offer returns that are not perfectly correlated, and so through asset diversification you can reduce the overall risk associated with investing.

Reminder!

See the following two examples for a better picture of how asset allocation affects a portfolio.

EXAMPLE #1: You have $20,000 in your portfolio.
- $15,000 (75%) is in the stock market
- $5,000 (25%) is kept in cash

During a stock market rally, the $15,000 invested in stocks increases to $20,000. Now, 80% of your total money is in the stock market instead of 75% and so cash comprises only 20% of your portfolio, increasing your risk to a future stock market decline because you are more "exposed" to stocks. If you want to keep the same *risk exposure*, you could sell off enough of the stock to return to your original asset allocation to 75% in stocks and 25% in cash.

EXAMPLE #2: You have $20,000 in your portfolio.
- $15,000 (75%) is in the stock market
- $5,000 (25%) is kept in cash

During a stock market decline, the $15,000 invested in stocks falls to $10,000. Now, only 66% of your portfolio is invested in stocks and so 33% is in cash, and so you have less chance of taking advantage of a stock market rally should one happen soon. If you want to keep the same *risk exposure*, you should buy more stock in order to return your original asset allocation to 75% stocks and 25% cash.

There is no "one size fits all" asset allocation. Everyone has different retirement goals and a different tolerance for the risk associated with investing. In general, however, the younger you are the greater percentage of stocks you should own in your portfolio. The reason for this is twofold. Because you have a longer time horizon, you can:
1) Make up for any temporary market losses due to downturns
2) Potentially take advantage of many years of investment growth

Reminder!

As you age, it is important to slowly scale back the amount of stocks you own and slowly increase the percentage of cash or cash equivalents in your overall portfolio. This will help to hedge against market downturns right when you begin needing the money in retirement.

A common equation to determine a typical percentage of stocks in a portfolio is as follows: 110 – your age. For example: if you are 30 years old, subtract 30 from 110, which = 80. Theoretically, therefore, an allocation of 80% stocks for a thirty-year-old is the recommended average. If you are 50 years old, subtract 50 from 110, which = 60, and that is the percentage of stocks recommended for someone of this age. While this is definitely NOT a hard and fast rule, it can give many typical investors a goal when determining an appropriate asset allocation regarding the amount of stocks to keep in a general portfolio.

Portfolio Management

It is important to manage all of your financial assets—retirement accounts, bank accounts, college savings accounts, emergency savings accounts, etc.—as a single portfolio. Knowing where all of your assets are and how they perform together as a group is essential if you wish to properly control your finances.

To begin, start to think about your portfolio in aggregate terms, not how each individual component or stock performs within the portfolio. For example, if one of the twenty stocks in your investment account loses 60% of its value in one year but your overall account grows by 12% because of gains in other stocks, you have made a substantial profit. This is true across your entire investment spectrum. For this reason, the asset allocation you chose is of utmost importance.

Another important part of portfolio management is simple knowledge. It may sound like common sense, but knowing something about your investments is imperative.

- If you do not know anything about a company, do not buy its stock or bonds.
- If you are unsure about what real estate is truly about, do not invest in it.
- If you cannot figure out what a certain mutual fund invests in, do not buy it.

Take the time to understand where you are putting your money, either through reading about potential investments yourself or through the explanations of a specialist or a certified financial planner that you trust. Since we all have different investment knowledge, we all therefore invest in different ways.

A final segment of portfolio management can be summed up by the following cliché: "Leave emotion at the door!" Many mutual funds and ETFs charge a fee when you both buy *and* sell them, and charge a fee every time you make a transaction within the fund. Money managers and stock funds also charge fees. Most of these investments have tax consequences when bought or sold as well.

Watch Out!

If you are constantly trying to "time" the market by getting in and out, you will lose substantial money in fees that erase any gains you might have experienced, even if the stock or fund grows in value.

Also, do not be sucked in by the talking heads of television news stations predicting either a financial Armageddon or the next hot area that guarantees results. Simply devise a plan and follow it, no matter what is happening around you. You will be glad you did. Rebalance your asset allocation at least once a year in order to make sure that the asset allocation is set at a desired place and stick to your original plan. Think LONG TERM, not next week.

Action Plan

Investing is perhaps the best legal way to experience significant returns on your money that does not include winning the lottery. If you have read this section about investing, hopefully you came away with enough knowledge to make an informed decision about which investment vehicles are right for you.

Reminder!

You should invest only when you are free of credit card debt AND you have an emergency savings account that is fully funded with at least six months' worth of living expenses.

For most people, investing in the stock market is the most common form of investing. This includes investing in individual stocks, mutual funds, index funds, ETFs, REITs, and other sectors of the market. Unfortunately, the current number of stocks on the various U.S. exchanges now number more than 10,000, while the total number of American mutual funds and ETFs has reached over 12,000. Add these numbers to the various stock exchanges across the world and the options in which to invest literally become almost endless. It is these many options that can completely confuse a novice investor. For many, picking what to invest in, then, is akin to finding a four-leaf clover hidden in a very large meadow. How do you know where to even begin looking?

There are a few basic rules that most investors should follow that will simultaneously reduce your risk exposure and, more importantly, make you money. Follow these guidelines and you will increase your chances of future profit:

- **You do not need an expensive money manager or stock broker.** They often charge large commissions that eat into your earnings and simply cannot guarantee superior results. They can dazzle you with past results and try to convince you to use their company or investment vehicles, but in the end many are little more than salesmen selling a product. As a general rule, however, if you have a complicated estate plan, a significant sum of money that you would like to invest, or desire to explore some of the more complicated investment vehicles, it is wise to consult a professional. Otherwise, you can do all the investing you need using only your home computer and this guide.

- **Smart investing is not glamorous.** Smart investors do not chase hot stock tips or put value in the ever-changing recommendations of the daily business news. Smart investors do not try to time the market by buying and selling stocks when markets go up or down. Smart investors have a long-term plan and stick to it, leaving emotion at the door.

- **Equaling the average market returns will make you money.** Sure, there are financial experts whose returns in hedge funds and mutual funds beat the average returns of the market sometimes. But over the course of a thirty-year time horizon, there is not a single money manager who has ever out-paced the overall market. If you stick to investing in an index fund tied to the S&P 500 or Russell 5000, you will always be guaranteed to roughly equal the market's return. No money manager or stock broker on the planet can guarantee that.

- **Keeping at least 5% of your portfolio in cash is a very good idea.** This can hedge against market downturns and give investors a little peace of mind. During drawn-out stock market declines, keeping 20% or more of a portfolio in cash is common. Your money should be in a high-yield savings account, a money market account, or a money market mutual fund that garners the most interest possible, ideally at least 3%. These types of accounts are generally insured by your bank as well. Check out some of the online banks listed in the Action Plan of the Savings chapter for places that usually pay greater interest than standard banks.

  o NOTE: Cash in your emergency savings account does not count toward an investment portfolio. The cash in emergency savings is to be used only for its stated purpose, while cash in an investment account is there to hedge against market drops and provide a holding sport for future material investments.

- **Bonds lose money when compared to stocks in the long term.** For an investor with a broad time horizon of at least ten years, bonds should be avoided.

- **Gold and silver are not great stores of value over time, but they provide stability to a portfolio.** While the monetary gains of gold and silver do not increase as rapidly as average stock market returns do, they provides great stability to a portfolio.

- **Every six months to twelve months check out your portfolio and rebalance it if necessary.** This means that as the market dramatically increases or decreases, the percentages you had elected to keep in stocks or mutual funds or cash might be different than what you originally desired. You need to rebalance in order to maintain your asset allocation in its original or desired proportions. As previously mentioned, the institutions at which you keep you money or investments probably have online or phone support to help guide you through this process.

- **Do not lose sight of the long term!** A smart investor thinks in the long term, not the short term. Write down your goals ("Retire at age 50" or "Contribute $50 per month to my Emergency Savings"). This includes never losing sight of the long term during market downturns or upswings: they will both happen again. For example, in the eighteen months leading up to March 2009, stocks sank to 12-year lows, erasing all of the impressive gains of the previous decade. But after this market low, stocks rebounded and gained back nearly 70% of their lost value in the next year. The smart investor knows that despite downturns, markets do rise and when they do, only those *invested in the market* will reap the gains.

- **Use a money-managing program.** There are many programs available to help you track your finances and investments. These programs require you to enter your financial information, like bank account numbers, stock and bond allocations, checking and saving account information, credit card information, etc. Then, through a series of intuitive and generally easy-to-understand graphs and diagrams, you can see all of your financial accounts in one place. These programs also often offer suggestions for ways to improve your financial situation by analyzing your information. Perhaps the most popular of these programs are *Quicken* (www.quicken.com) and *Microsoft Money* (www.microsoft.com/money). Both programs cost between $40 and $100, depending on which version you choose. There are also numerous free programs online, the best being MINT (www.mint.com). All are solid programs and employ numerous web-based security features to ensure your online safety. Open an account today and see where all of your money is. Then, follow the advice in this section about what to invest in and how to allocate your money.

Using all of the strategies in this Action Plan will greatly aid you in your money management. And because investing is closely linked to retirement, you are helping yourself achieve your dreams by following the advice herein. In the end, we all invest and save money so that one day we can live well in retirement and enjoy our golden years in peace and tranquility. Understanding how to do that is imperative. Employ the practices listed in this chapter regarding *how* to invest as you plan for retirement so that one day you *can* retire and live the way you have always wanted.

Chapter Five:

To Buy Or To Rent?

To Buy Or To Rent?

For many people, buying a home is the ultimate form of personal and financial satisfaction. Indeed, the ownership of a home has become a status symbol of the realization of the grand American Dream. You can own the property your home sits on and everything in it, decorating it and painting it in any way that you would like. It provides not only shelter from the elements but also your very own piece of the world that no one can take away.

The problem is that the U.S. economy massively imploded during the recession of 2007-2009, partly as a result of people not knowing how much "house" they could afford. Today, literally hundreds of thousands of people have declared personal bankruptcy because they cannot afford the home they live in. And millions more face home foreclosure because they did not have the money to buy a house but did so anyway.

The surge of easily available credit in the early part of the past decade meant that people with no money in the bank could borrow huge amounts of capital, and buy a home worth far more than they could afford. In the end, many people could not meet the monthly mortgage payments due on their home and either faced foreclosure, refinance for even longer-term repayment terms, or had to take on additional mortgages, putting themselves further into debt. It has been a vicious downward spiral.

Having said this, however, owning a home can be an important part of any financial plan. This chapter, though, is not a "how-to" guide about buying a home. There are countless books and articles devoted to the specifics regarding how to go about actually buying a home. There are also thousands of web pages devoted solely to the purchasing and owning of a home. If you want a guide that will take you through the step-by-step process of buying your dream house, check out your local bookstore or search online.

This chapter, conversely, helps delineate the reasons *why* you should or should not purchase a home. Like other sections of this book, this chapter focuses on developing good financial practices. With solid financial knowledge, an informed buyer can decide if it right to purchase a home now or wait until more capital is acquired. In other words, can you *afford* to buy a home?

This is perhaps a far more important discussion topic than the more typical "*How* to buy a home" conversation. For many people, knowing if they can afford to purchase a home is one of the most important financial decisions that exist.

If you are pondering home ownership, carefully read the essentials listed on the following pages and weigh the information presented in each part. It will give you a solid base in your decision-making process and hopefully help you determine if home ownership is right for you at this point in you life or not. Once this important decision is made, then you can start the *how to* discussion. Good luck house hunting!

Buy a Home to Stay Put

You should only ever purchase a home if you are in love with it, in love with the area, and can see yourself staying put for a minimum of five years. Ideally, you will buy a home with the intent of remaining in it for many, many years.

Watch Out!

Many people buy homes and then decide to move a year or two later. They bought a home because "everybody buys a home." This is the wrong reason to do so.

If you can commit to remaining in your home for at least a half-decade and you would enjoy living there for even longer than this, then you can begin thinking about owning a home. The reasons behind this are simple:

- Given all of the transaction costs associated with buying a home, sometimes totaling $20,000 or more, it can take a while to recoup this money; often, this amount is not included in the purchase price or as a part of the decision-making process.

- If you purchase a home and then sell it within a few years, you may end up losing a significant sum of money if the value of your home has declined (as it did for millions of people during the housing bubble bursting of 2006-8).

- You are not guaranteed to find a buyer right away who wants you home!

Therefore, because of the above reasons and numerous others, only consider buying a home if you intend to stay put for an extended period of time. If you only plan to live in the house for a couple years, you will eat into any home appreciation (assuming you have some) with all of the costs associated when purchasing a property. But if you can reasonably assert that you would like to remain in the house and the area for at least five years and, ideally, a decade or more, then you can begin further thinking about home ownership.

Consider this last note: Many people buy homes as an investment. This means that they do not intend to live in the home, but instead plan to buy it and sell it quickly for more money than they originally paid. For more information about investing in real estate—as opposed to buying a home to live in—see the section about real estate and REITs in the preceding "Investing" chapter.

Paying for a Home

One of the primary reasons why our economy experienced such a significant downturn in the past few years is because too many people had previously purchased homes with essentially no down payment. They could not afford the traditional 20% as one lump-sum down payment, so put down 5% or 10% only. Sometimes, people found ways to buy homes with a down payment of nothing. Imagine buying a home for $300,000 and mortgaging the entire thing because you could not even afford a small portion to put down! Thus, how can you afford the rest of the house?

At the height of the real estate upswing from 2002-2006, however, small down payments did not seem to matter for many buyers or for many lenders. This is because real estate prices were increasing so fast that you could buy a home with no money down and reasonably expect the overall value of the home to increase so rapidly that you would end up gaining substantial equity and making a profit if you sold it a just couple years later.

Reminder!

Just as home prices can rise, so can they fall. And because thousands of people had no equity in their home because they could not afford even a meager down payment, they fell behind on payments and faced foreclosure and even bankruptcy.

Further, with the increase in popularity of adjustable rate mortgages during this time, people could buy a home—again, with little or no down payment—and would owe a very low interest payment for the first few years of the mortgage. Because home values had recently increased so drastically, many people thought that by the time their mortgage rate re-adjusted they would have built up enough equity that they could afford the higher rates and payments. But, as everyone already knows, the housing bubble killed this idea and many people subsequently lost their homes. Simply, they could not afford the house in which they were living.

Money Goal!

The absolute rule is to put down 20% of the home's price when you purchase it. If you cannot do this, do not consider buying a home right now. Start saving.

Additionally, many people do not realize the actual cost of owning a home over time without a large down payment upfront. Consider the following example.

EXAMPLE: You purchase a home for $100,000 but can only afford a 10% down payment ($10,000) with a 30-year mortgage. This means that you need to finance the remaining $90,000 over the next thirty years as a mortgage. At an industry-average 7% mortgage rate, your $100,000 home will end up costing you nearly $230,000 by the time you have paid off what you owe. In other words, you will pay *more* than the actual value of your house in interest payments! The larger the down payment at the outset, though, the less interest you pay.

Here is another warning against not having sufficient money to make a responsible home purchase: with a down payment under 20%, you will legally be required to have private mortgage insurance (PMI). PMI is a safety net that protects the bank in case you fail to make payments. PMI can add about 0.5% of the total loan amount to your mortgage payments for the year, which does not sound like much but can really add up.

Let's say you finance a $100,000 mortgage. Your PMI will probably cost between $300 and $600 annually, which significantly increases your monthly payments. For this reason as well, you should always have at least 20% of the home's purchase price as a down payment. If you do not, buying a home right now is not for you.

Moreover, the larger your down payment, the shorter your mortgage can be. If you can afford a reasonable down payment, you may perhaps be able to have a fifteen-year mortgage. This will dramatically decrease the amount of money you pay in interest over the life of the mortgage.

To illustrate this, consider the example of a home purchased for $150,000 at 7% interest.

- For a traditional thirty-year mortgage, you will pay nearly $175,000 in interest alone, bringing your total to $325,000.
- For a traditional fifteen-year mortgage, you will pay only about $75,000 in interest, bringing your total to only $225,000.

As you can see, this is a dramatic difference ($100,000 in interest payments alone!). Additionally, interest rates on shorter-term mortgages are usually lower than those on longer-term ones anyway, sometimes by a full percentage point or more, thus lowering your actual monthly payments and total purchase price even further. Therefore, the difference between the final outcomes in the above example would actually be even greater, in favor of the fifteen-year mortgage. The savings over the life of the mortgage would literally be equal to the entire cost of the house itself.

In the end, then, if you cannot afford a sizeable down payment, you are not ready to buy a house yet. Keep saving until you can safely put down at least 20% of the purchase price. Also, remember how dramatic the differences are between having a fifteen- versus a thirty-year mortgage.

The shorter the mortgage term, the less you pay in interest to the bank. This means you keep more money.

Emergency Savings and Down Payments

Once you have determined that you have enough money to afford at least 20% down and the monthly payments on a short mortgage rather than one that is three decades long or more, there is one more thing to consider: emergency savings and down payments.

Say you have been financially diligent and have finished paying off all credit card debt and have built a six-month emergency savings fund. You think that you are doing well financially and decide that now is the time to buy a home. This is the wrong thought process!

Watch Out!

Spending your entire emergency savings account on a down payment is very unwise. Six months' worth of savings is gone and you now have no money saved in case an actual emergency befalls you.

What happens if you lose your job next month? What happens if you have an auto accident that leaves you bed-ridden for a year? What if your child needs a set of $3000 braces that are not covered by insurance? What happens if a parent needs financial support that you were not planning on? Your shiny new house with the down payment is great, but if you cannot afford to buy groceries or any other of life's necessities, the house does you little good.

Being able to afford a down payment of at least 20% of the purchase price of a home means that you have this much money saved *in addition to* your regular savings. Only then should you consider buying a home.

Aim For a Home You Can Actually Afford

Too many people decide that they need to buy a home and that it has to be at least as big as their co-worker's home (see the "Blame Thy Neighbors" section in the "Saving" chapter of this guide for more on this). But you should only ever buy a home that is as much *as you can afford*.

A generally-accepted rule of thumb is that most people can afford to buy a house that costs about no more than three times their household annual salary. This means that if you earn $50,000 per year and plan to buy a house, a top starting-price should be in the $150,000 range. If you earn $125,000 per year, you can probably afford a house costing roughly $375,000. This is merely a general estimate, however, and not a hard and fast rule. Everyone's situation is different. But be sure to remember that you must be *able* to afford this amount (no debt, fully-funded emergency savings, and 20% down ready to go) before you are even allowed to think about going forward with buying a home.

There are many "home purchase" calculators available online to help you get a better handle on how your income, debts, and expenses affect what you can afford as far as home ownership. Check out the following websites that help you calculate approximately how much "home" you can afford:

- http://www.mortgage101.com/affordability-calculator
- http://money.cnn.com/pf/loan_center/index.html

For a more accurate figure, though, ask to be pre-approved by a commercial lender, who will look at your income, your FICO score (discussed in the next section), your available credit, and other factors to determine the kind and size of the loan that would fit your situation.

One final rule when calculating if you can or cannot afford a home right now: all of your monthly home payments (including property taxes, PMI, utilities, mortgage payment, etc.) should never exceed 33% of your gross monthly income. Ideally, you should try to keep your total home-related payments under 30% of your monthly income (This would apply to rental pricing as well). If you are going to pay more than this 30% or so, the house you plan on buying is more than you can afford. Consider buying a smaller house, getting a smaller loan, or continue renting until you can afford a larger down payment (which will equate to smaller monthly payments).

FICO scores

The accepted benchmark for a very large portion of your financial portfolio is your FICO score. More than anything, though, your FICO score affects the approvability and interest for any loans you take on.

In particular, your FICO score might be perhaps the single most important number indicating your financial record. Most people do not realize how essential it is to their overall financial health. In fact, employers can check your FICO score; credit card companies can check your FICO score; commercial lenders can check your FICO score; car dealerships can check your FICO score; the IRS can check your FICO score; your bank can check your FICO score. And the list goes on.

Simply defined, a FICO score is an assigned three-digit number that represents your *credit worthiness*. The word FICO is an acronym derived from the credit model developed in the 1950s by the Fair Isaac Corporation.

Everyone's FICO score is reported by the three central credit reporting companies: TransUnion, Equifax, and Experian. FICO scores range from 300 to 900, though most people have scores between 600 and 800. The higher your score is, the better rates you can get. FICO scores depend on a number of factors, which include the following (listed in approximate order of importance):

- Payment history
    - o Have you normally been on time or late for payments on credit cards and other loans?
- Length of payment history
    - o How long have you had credit cards?
- Amount and usage of available credit
    - o What is the total credit limit on all of your credit cards? Experts recommend never exceeding 50% of your total credit.
- Debt-to-credit ratio
    - o How much debt do you have total (credit cards, student or car loans, etc.) compared to your available credit?
- Loan and employment history
    - o The more responsible you have been in the past, the better your future rates.

- Number of credit card openings and closures
  - o If you constantly open and close cards, this negatively affects credit score.

Each year, all Americans are entitled to view their credit report once from each of the three credit reporting agencies mentioned above. To do this, go to the following website and follow the online instructions:

www.annualcreditreport.com

It is a good idea to check your credit reports every year to ensure that there are no mistakes or misinformation. Many people who regularly monitor their credit reports find errors occasionally, and unfortunately it is no one's responsibility to do this but you.

It is also a good idea to know your approximate score so you can notice any changes in it that seem out of line, which can signify a case of stolen identity or a stolen credit card. In short, having knowledge of your finances includes knowing about your FICO score.

There are many other websites that can give you credit reports, but the above site is the only one that is sanctioned by the government and federally endorsed.

Watch Out!

Some companies participate in lots of television and internet advertising to lure viewers to their websites. You should not use these other sites because they sign you up automatically for credit "protection" programs that charge a monthly fee and are difficult to cancel.

Many of these other sites are also more expensive than the federally-endorsed website. Thus, only get your credit report from the official, government-sponsored site listed above and do this every year.

Since you most likely will need to get a mortgage to buy a house, you must make sure that your credit history is also as clean as possible. A few months before you start house hunting, therefore, get copies of your credit reports from the three central agencies and make sure that the facts are correct. If you find any errors, make sure to call the agency to fix them right away. This is a time-consuming and tedious process, but a necessary one.

For additional information regarding your FICO score, a great website devoted to helping you understand everything involved regarding FICO scores and credit reporting is

- http://www.myfico.com.

This website does not provide actual FICO scores, but instead offers lots of advice about FICO scores in general.

Schools, Crime, and Sidewalks

Too many people never check out the following three important areas when buying a home: schools, crime, and sidewalks. All three are essential parts of the research you should conduct when gearing up to buy a home and deciding if you should purchase it or not.

Even if you do not have school-aged children, good schools boost the value of all homes in the area and should be an integral part of your buying decision.

Reminder!

If you decide to move out of your home years from now, future buyers might have young children and the quality of schools will matter greatly to them. Or, perhaps more importantly, you might have school-age children some day and want a reputable place to send them. The schools where you plan to buy a house must be good or you should look elsewhere.

A neighborhood's crime rate is also an important factor. To determine crime in an area, perhaps the most productive way is to buy a local newspaper and peruse the different sections: look for crime reports and any local arrests.

Also, do a quick online search of the neighborhood or town in general. Look at the type of neighborhood and any houses or buildings in it. It is mostly residential with well-kept houses or more commercial with many businesses nearby? Are there liquor shops and 24-hour convenience stores or nice family-oriented boutiques?

Finally, it is a very good idea to drive through a future neighborhood late at night, preferably after 11:00pm on a Friday or Saturday. Check out what the street corners look like and if there are any places that might attract late-night hangouts. Perhaps the best advice here is to use your gut feeling: would you want your 15-year-old daughter walking by herself here at night? If not, perhaps this is not the area in which you want to buy a home.

A third and final often-overlooked factor in home buying decisions involves the sidewalks. Sidewalks normally do not attract much attention and are often passed over. But the first time you want to take your kids for a walk in a stroller or want to take a romantic stroll or rollerblade through the neighborhood with your wife or girlfriend, you will be glad to have flat, well-manicured sidewalks on the streets around your home.

So when you consider buying a home, also take a walk around the neighborhood to look at the sidewalks to see what kind of shape they are in. If you are in a big city, do you even have sidewalks near your future house? This might affect whether you want to buy a house or condo there.

In sum, therefore, the three key areas discussed in this section should comprise at least a portion of your decision about whether or not the area is a good place to look for a house. They do not necessarily influence if you can afford to buy a home, but are so often overlooked in the decision-making process that it seems relevant to mention them in this guide.

Action Plan

Saving for a home is a big step in any financial plan. Unfortunately, many people rush into purchasing a home and spend far too much money before they are ready to do so, severely hurting their financial health. Consider the recent financial crisis that affected this country and the information that shoddy home purchasing decision-making was one of the primary culprits.

> Simply put, you should never, ever consider buying a home if you cannot afford it, plain and simple.

If you cannot afford to buy a home based on the information provided in this book, you can rent for a while longer and everything will work out fine. Many people rent for their whole lives, which is also fine. While buying a home can be a great thing and provides stability, tax breaks, and a sense of permanence, ruining your financial future to buy a house before you are ready is a bad idea indeed.

When you do decide to purchase a home, though, follow this line of thinking, as discussed in this chapter:

- Make sure that you have no damaging credit card debt at high interest rates that is dramatically hurting your credit score and your finances
- Make sure you have at least 20% of the purchase price set aside for a down payment that will NOT drain your emergency savings
- Make sure you take into account that all of the closing costs associated with purchasing a home, which can sometimes approach a hefty 6-8% of the total purchase price, require a significant chunk of money to be paid in addition to the down payment and are required at the time of purchase
- Make sure that your mortgage payments and all relevant home expenses do not exceed 33% of your total monthly income
- Make sure that you do your best to secure a good interest rate for your mortgage, and that it is for as short a time as can comfortably be afforded (remember from the example how much more a person pays with a traditional 30-year vs. a 15-year fixed-rate mortgage)

If you can meet all of these criteria, you are ready to begin the home-buying (or thinking-of-home-buying) process. As previously mentioned, there are scores of books and magazines in your local bookstore that can take you through the many steps involved in finding and buying a home that you like. Just remember that very few of these resources actually make you decide whether or not you can *afford* to buy a home. That is the first, and perhaps the most important, step in the whole process.

Chapter Six:

Retirement

Retirement

etirement is a very special time. To some, it is the end of a long journey; to others, it is just the beginning. It can begin at any age and extend for decades. It can happen to those in declining health and advancing age, or to those in great health and at a young age. Retirement, for many, is the much-anticipated arrival of peace and leisure time to enjoy with friends and family.

For most of us, getting to retirement involves a lifetime of saving, investing, and careful financial planning. We work for years and hopefully have diligently accumulated enough assets to allow us to cease running the rat race and enjoy life. This is not the reality for many, however.

Watch Out!

The truth to how many Americans plan for retirement can be witnessed by walking into nearly any department store or fast-food establishment: you will see an army of "over-70s" working behind cash registers, re-stocking shelves, and organizing row after row of cheap apparel.

As a famous case in point, Wal-mart has carved out a rather infamous reputation of employing the elderly to function as "greeters" who give a quick salutation at the door to all those entering the massive low-cost chain.

Many older Americans, simply, cannot afford to live out their glory years without supplementing their meager Social Security benefits. Some suffer through leg and back pain, substantial joint arthritis, and complete exhaustion just to receive a minimum-wage paycheck from these department stores and fast-food restaurants. But, if at age 84 you are in need of money, few decent or upscale places will hire you, so your options are extremely (and sadly) limited. If you plan well, however, this increasingly common image does not have to have you in it. Read the rest of this chapter carefully and it will explain some retirement basics and help you to live your dreams with enough money to spend and then some.

Understanding "Traditional" Retirement

Until only quite recently, retirement in the United States used to be a fairly simple and straightforward process. Retirees had two guaranteed sources of income that had always provided enough on which to live: a pension and Social Security. Both are discussed below.

Pensions

Most people used to work at the same job for all of their adult lives. As a thank you for many years of company loyalty, job devotion, and cheerful service, your employer—which had been putting aside money for you diligently into a big pension trust fund—gave you a pension check every month for the rest of your life. You received the check no matter how well or poorly the economy did. In fact, employers used to be required by company mandate to keep their pension trust funds fully supplied so as not to run out of money during economic downturns. And many employers even continued sending a pension check every month to your spouse after your death.

A pension's benefits used to be defined by your job experience and salary using a simple actuarial formula. It was often also written into your work contract, to be depended upon entirely. Thus, this type of pension is often called a *defined benefit* plan. For most of the 20th century, a person's retirement usually consisted primarily of this pension system.

A recent problem with this type of plan, though, is that people are living longer after retiring, so receive more monthly checks and thus cost the company more money. Additionally, there are a huge number of retiring baby boomers right now, many more than was expected; all of these people would also need pension checks if this system had continued. Therefore, today more and more companies are unfortunately shying away from that traditional staple of retirement income, the pension.

Social Security

Social Security, the other tier of a traditional retirement, began in 1935 as a federal agency to help fund the post-work of government employees, and soon expanded to include most of the U.S. workforce. It pays retirees an accrued average of their thirty-five highest-income earning years, based on their tax returns. The maximum monthly Social Security check that you can earn is currently capped at a fixed dollar amount, however, regardless of income.

Today, the Social Security program is in trouble. Although current retirees continue to receive their monthly checks, this government program has deep schisms that severely threaten its continued existence.

To begin with, the advent of nearly 80 million baby boomers quickly approaching retirement age will soon force the Social Security trust fund to be more heavily drawn upon than ever before in its history. Couple this with the loss of a massive number of employees about to leave the workforce, which will reduce the funding of the Social Security trust fund, and the program is in trouble indeed.

Despite what many people believe, Social Security is not a system in which a small portion of your paycheck is deposited and saved for you by the federal government until you retire, at which point in time you start receiving those contributions back until you die. It is not a savings account.

The Social Security system instead works like a "pay-as-you-go" system, meaning that money paid in Social Security taxes by current workers goes toward paying the benefits of today's current retirees. Each generation of workers accordingly funds the preceding generation's elder non-working years.

As the ratio of current workers to current retirees drops, though, the system will undoubtedly fail. Not only will fewer current workers be paying into the system, but a larger number of retirees will be receiving withdrawals from it. Essentially, the system is under-funded and over-withdrawn.

In addition, due to recent medical advances, people today are living much longer than when the Social Security program first began. This requires additional checks to every recipient, further stretching out the payments that millions of Americans receive today or will be receiving in the future.

In the end, then, even the most optimistic projections have the Social Security trust fund running dry within a few decades, and some people predict that it will fall short much sooner. At some point, all retirees will only receive a small portion of what the program dictates they should receive.

With these two traditional retirement programs—pensions and Social Security—for most of the past century workers have been adequately covered in retirement and have usually given little thought to funding their own golden years.

The problem is that today few U.S. companies offer defined pensions to new employees and many of those people receiving pensions currently have seen their payouts reduced or even cut due to a struggling economy. With only a few exceptions, the pension as 20th-century America knew it is now defunct and Social Security might be on the brink of becoming so.

Retirement Basics Today

It is obvious that the two primary historical pillars of retirement income, pensions and Social Security, are running dry and cannot be depended upon for years into the future. This is especially true for post-baby boomer generations, sometimes referred to as "Generation X" (born between 1960-1980) and "Generation Y" (born between 1980-2000).

Our country now expects people to provide for themselves in retirement. Because of this, numerous new retirement income sources have originated. In particular, the last two decades have seen the surging of Individual Retirement Accounts (IRAs), while most companies have also switched from a traditional pension plan system to an employee-funded *defined-contribution* plan (including 401(k) and 403(b) plans). All of these retirement account types are explained in the following pages.

Reminder!

An important thing to remember as you are reading this chapter about retirement is that "retirement" does not need to mean "old." You can retire at any age if you have the financial means to do so!

Most people stop working when they are in their 60s or older because they cannot *afford* to retire earlier; simply, they would not have enough money saved and invested to permit an absence of a regular salary. The reality, though, is that it does not matter when you retire, whether that is 25, 45, 65, or 85 years old. If you can support yourself through your savings and investments for many years without working, you can stop to savor and enjoy life without alarm clocks, board meetings, bosses, and cubicles.

Your retirement is closely linked to your investment portfolio. Indeed, for many people a sizable portion of their invested assets exist within one of the various types of retirement accounts. As you read through this section on retirement, think about how you can use your knowledge of investing to help make enough money so that "early" retirement is not merely a fantasy reserved for the super rich, but instead a reality that anyone can achieve!

But how do you know when you have enough saved and invested to retire? How do you know how much money you'll need to stop working? The answer lies in a very simple math equation that any fifth grader could figure out. In the next section, we take you through how to determine when you have enough saved and invested to retire.

Annual Income Requirement

Your Annual Income Requirement (AIR) will be referred to throughout this section. It is a very important tool to use as you start thinking about your financial situation and retiring some day.

Simply, your AIR is the amount of money you need each year to live on. For most of us, our AIR is roughly equivalent to our yearly salary: we receive the majority of our income from our jobs and so this is about how much money we spend.

To figure out your AIR:
- Record all of your expenses for an entire month in a journal or spreadsheet.
- Include everything you spend money on, down to the finest detail:
    o Your rent
    o All food expenses (even small snacks, bubble gum, a late-night drink, and your daily coffee)
    o Your trip to the movies
    o All of your insurance (car, home, property, etc.)
    o Your cell phone bill

- o Your cable bill
- o A splurge birthday present for your best friend
- o And everything else you spend money on.
- Once you spend an entire month recording your expenses, multiply this number by 12 to reflect your yearly expenses.
- Lastly, add $5,000 to your total 12-month sum to cover any additional miscellaneous expenses.
- This final number is your AIR.

Below is an actual mathematical example that will illustrate the above steps:

1) After a full month of diligent recording, you find out that your total monthly expenses = $2,500
2) $2,500 per month x 12 = $30,000
3) $30,000 + $5,000 = $35,000
4) Your AIR = $35,000

It is important to know your AIR because it is the jumping off point to determine how much you will need in terms of monetary assets to be able to retire from your job while you are still vibrant enough to enjoy traveling, hobbies, and spending time with friends and family.

To determine how much money you need total in order to retire comfortably, use the following formula:

Financial Independence = AIR x 25

The reason why this formula works is simple: If you can determine your AIR, which tells you how much money you will need each year to live on, then you can figure out how much money you will need saved and invested to allow you to retire comfortably. The reason why we multiply our AIR by 25 is to give us a total retirement or investment portfolio from which we can safely withdraw about 4% a year (or 1/25th) and not face a great risk of future complete portfolio depletion.

By way of continuing our previous example, the following steps will illustrate how to arrive at your "Financial Independence" number:

- Recall your AIR ($35,000)
- Multiply this number by 25
- Now you have your financial goal of $825,000

- o $35,000 \times 25 = 875,000$
- o You need this amount saved and invested to have acquired financial independence.
- For some additional examples, see below:
  - o If your AIR = $20,000, your financial goal = $500,000
  - o If your AIR = $50,000, your financial goal = $1.25 million
  - o If your AIR = $80,000, your financial goal = $2.0 million
  - o If your AIR = $130,000, your financial goal = $3.25 million

The point of all of this is simple: Determine your AIR and then strive—through financial investments and work that you enjoy—to have 25 times that number saved up and invested. When you do this, and it can take many decades of diligent work, you will have achieved true financial independence.

Individual Retirement Accounts (IRAs)

An Individual Retirement Account is an investment account whose funds are earmarked for (or applied toward) retirement only. There are numerous types of IRAs available to investors, and all offer distinct tax advantages. Unlike 401(k)s and 403(b)s, which are discussed in the next section of this chapter, IRAs are entirely investor-funded and investor-directed. This means that if you want to have an IRA, you must open one yourself and not rely on your employer to open it for you.

Money Goal!

IRAs are perhaps the greatest way to save for retirement because they offer total control of the account, tax breaks, and are easy to open and direct. If you do not already have one, open one today after you have read this section.

One of the many advantages of an IRA is that you maintain 100% control over how to direct the money inside the account. You can pick any investment you want and not be constrained by workplace rules or the limited investment options often applied by workplace retirement accounts.

Investing in an IRA is not as hard as it seems, though. By following the investment advice from the preceding chapter on the money *within* your IRA, you have all the tools necessary to invest with confidence and productivity. As you open one, consider the following general rules about IRAs:

- You can contribute any amount up to $5,000 during each fiscal year if you have earned income greater than that amount. You do not need to contribute all of this at once, but instead can deposit the money bit by bit during the course of the year.
- All contributions to an IRA must be made in cash. You cannot contribute property or stocks to an IRA.
- You may not take out money from an IRA before age 59½ without incurring an "Early Withdrawal" penalty, except in a few very specific circumstances. A few of these circumstances are discussed later on in this section.
- Once you open an IRA, you do not need to fund it every year if you do not have enough money to do so, although you definitely should if possible.
- If you are married, each member of the couple can have his or her own IRA.

There are two main types of IRAs available to investors. These two types of IRAs function in a similar fashion regarding how you invest money within them, but they are funded differently, have different tax consequences, and impose certain contribution restrictions. Each is discussed in the following pages.

Traditional IRA

A traditional IRA was for a long time the only type of IRA available to the average investor. In a Traditional IRA, all contributions are tax-deferred, meaning that you pay no taxes on money when you deposit it. For many investors, this fact is a wonderful benefit. If you are in a high tax bracket, contributing to a Traditional IRA not only helps you save for retirement, but lessens your taxable income.

By way of example, let's say that you make $85,000 per year from your job. Consider the following:

- You are in the 28% tax bracket, which means that you pay roughly $24,000 per year in federal income taxes.
- This leaves your "take-home" pay (disregarding state taxes) at about $61,000 per year.
- If you decided to contribute $5,000 to a Traditional IRA, though, this amount is deducted from your original taxable income.
- According to the IRS, your "new" taxable income is now only $80,000 per year. You have just moved down into the 25% tax bracket, which means you pay only $20,000 per year in federal income taxes, leaving your "take-home" pay at about $60,000.
- In the end, by contributing $5,000 to a Traditional IRA you have not only saved that amount for retirement, but will also pay about $4,000 less in taxes for the year. Your total take-home pay is only $1,000 less even though you contributed $5,000 to a retirement account. The government basically let you have $4,000 in free money.

Traditional IRAs are a good way to save for retirement because of the tax breaks they offer when you deposit money. You do, though, have to pay regular taxes on the money and all of your earnings when you withdraw the money in retirement. But for many people, when they retire they are in a lower tax bracket, lessening the amount of total taxes paid.

Roth IRA

Roth IRAs are the other type of IRA available to most investors. Originating in 1996, Roth IRAs are perhaps the most phenomenal investment choice available to most Americans. The reason for this is simple: all contributions to it are after-tax, which means that all earnings grow tax-free and all future withdrawals are tax free. Yes, TAX FREE!

The government has imposed certain restrictions on contributing to a Roth IRA, which are summarized below:

- As a single tax filer, you may only contribute to a Roth IRA if your Adjusted Gross Income (AGI) for the fiscal year is below $105,000 (you can contribute a lesser amount than the full $5,000 if your AGI is between $105,000 and $120,000, after which you are ineligible to contribute).
- If you are married and filing taxes jointly, you may contribute to a Roth IRA if your household AGI is below $166,000 (you can contribute a lesser amount than the full $5,000 for an AGI below $176,000, after which you are ineligible to contribute).
- After a Roth IRA has been open for five years, any principal you add during the life of the account can always be withdrawn free from penalties – forever. For example, if you decide you need some additional money as a down payment for a house and have a significant sum already in your Roth IRA, eligible principal that you have contributed in the past can be withdrawn and used penalty-free (even if you are younger than (59½). While this act would clearly go against why you are saving for retirement in the first place, it is there as an option should you need it.
- Also, Roth IRAs do not have mandatory withdrawals like some other retirement accounts do, so if you do not spend all of the money in your IRA before you die, you can leave it to your children or grandchildren and they can also enjoy its many benefits and continue to experience growth in the account.
- All principal growth and all earnings can be withdrawn tax free from a Roth IRA when you reach age 59½. TAX FREE.

If you do not already have an IRA and are eligible, open one immediately and start contributing (if, of course, you have no credit card debt and already have a fully-funded emergency savings account). In particular, if you qualify for a Roth IRA it is a great idea to take advantage of the many benefits that this type of account offers.

For more detailed information on some other types of IRAs (including IRAs for those that are self-employed), go to the following website:

- http://www.IRA.com

This website has detailed information about all types of IRAs and can further help you decide which one may be right for you.

401(k) and 403(b)

Many Americans are lucky enough to work for an employer that sponsors a *defined-contribution* retirement plan. Defined-contribution plans are becoming increasingly popular because they free employers from the constricting—and very costly—pension system and offer tax-deferred earnings growth to employees. This means that contributions and earnings are not taxed until they are withdrawn at retirement, at which time many people are in a lower tax bracket. In this way, this type of retirement plan has many of the same tax benefits as a Traditional IRA.

There are two basic types of defined-contribution plans: a 401(k) and a 403(b), both named after the IRS tax code that governs them. These plans are essentially the same thing, the only difference being that a 403(b) is offered at non-profit institutions like schools, hospitals, charities, and other aid organizations, while a 401(k) is offered at for-profit institutions and businesses.

Because the days of fixed pensions are generally gone, defined-contribution plans (also called "employee-directed" plans), are often the only source of retirement funds for many Americans.

Reminder!

There are many benefits to 401(k)s and 403(b)s, which will be discussed in the following pages, but there are also a few drawbacks. First and foremost, unlike a traditional pension, today employees are now fully responsible for the direction and funding of their own retirement accounts. While "matching" programs from employers exist (which will also be covered later in this section), the general contributions and organization of the account rests with you, the worker.

Another drawback to this defined-contribution system is that it comes with no guarantees of future success. As previously discussed, if you are the recipient of a standard pension, you receive your check every month for the rest of your life no matter what the economy does. With the new 401(k)s and 403(b)s, the burden is on the employee to put money into the account and manage it correctly. Thus, contributors are subject to the whims and gyrations of the stock and bond market.

But while there are these drawbacks, there are also many positive aspects to this new system. Most importantly, many companies "match" your monthly contributions to a 401(k) or 403(b). If you contribute 5% of your paycheck every month to an account, for example, your employer may also contribute an amount equal to your contribution. This matching is, for all intents and purposes, free money. You guarantee a 100% return on your contributed money right away because your 5% automatically becomes 10% the moment it enters the account. See the example below for a detailed explanation of how this works.

> EXAMPLE: You earn $40,000 per year from your job and contribute 5% of every paycheck to an employer-sponsored 401(k).
> - Your contributions total roughly $167 per month (or $2,000 per year based on the $40,000 salary).
> - You do not owe any taxes on this money because it is deposited pre-tax (you will only pay taxes on it when it is withdrawn in retirement).
> - Your total taxable income will decrease (like with Traditional IRA contributions) by the amount contributed, in this case $167 per month.
> - With a 5% company match, another $167 goes into the account every month in addition to your contribution (often, you only get to keep this money when you become "vested"—see the next section for an explanation).
> - Assuming that you also receive some market gains in your account, your $2,000 contributed per year can reasonably be expected to not only top $4,000, but will probably become

even more than that. This is more than a 100% return! Not a bad investment, indeed.

Another good aspect of this system is that you retain much more control of the money in your account than you would with a standard pension. You can choose to invest in stocks or bonds or mutual funds or anything you wish.

Further, many companies try to make it easy for employees to decide their investments by offering a few set options that reflect common investment styles, such as *Aggressive* (mostly stocks), *Moderate* (a balanced mix of stocks and bonds), and *Conservative* (more bonds than stocks). In short, with this 401(k) and 403(b) system, it is very easy to choose an investment strategy that is right for you. And in addition, nearly all companies offer 24-hour online support if you have questions about your account.

If your employer offers one of these accounts, sign up right away if you have not already and begin contributing. Also be sure to take advantage of a company match if one is offered.

What does "Being Vested" mean?

As discussed above, many companies now offer defined-contribution plans like 401(k)s and 403(b)s to their employees and have a company match. As an incentive to stay with a company, employees are often only eligible to keep a match after they become *vested*, which can be anywhere from one year to perhaps as long as six years.

What this means is that the company will match your salary in a certain percentage, like in our previous example, contributing that percentage to your account. But this money is yours to keep only after you work at the same institution until you become vested. Thus, if you decide to leave the company after two years and the vesting period is three years, you will get to keep any money that you have contributed personally to your retirement account, but the company will take back their share because you have not "earned" the money yet. It is to your benefit, therefore, to continue working at your company through the initial vest period in order to reap the rewards of your employer match.

There are different types of matching systems used during the vest period and beyond. Some use a "Cliff" system, in which you earn a 0% company match for the first year or two of employment, after which you get a 100% company match on your contributions after vesting.

Other companies use a "Graded" system, in which each year of service to the institution garners a higher match:

- In Year 1 you receive a 0% match
- In Year 2 you receive a 25% match
- In Year 3 you receive a 50% match
- In Year 4 you receive a 75% match
- In Year 5 you receive a 100% match

By way of a more concrete explanation of how the employer match/ vesting system works, see the following detailed example:

You contribute 5% of your $40,000 salary ($2,000 total per year) into a 401(k) and your employer—which has a three-year vesting period— matches you that same amount from your first day on the job. After the first year, you have $4,000 of principal (your $2,000 contribution and an equal company match of $2,000). Assuming a gain of 6% on the investments within your account, your total after Year 1 will be $4,240 ($4,000 principal + $240 [6%] in stock gains).

At the end of Year 2, assuming another year of 6% stock gains on the account, your money will grow as follows:

- Year 1 total + Year 2 principal ($4,000) = $8,240
- 6% gains on all of Year 2 ($8,240) = $494
- Total after Year 2 = $8,240 + $494 = $8,734

If you leave the company now, however, you have not reached the end of your vest period and your employer will take back its $4,000 of contributed money. Plus, they will also take back their share of the 6% gains. Your account will fall to only $4,367. This money—what you personally contributed—is still yours to keep, no matter what. But it is only half as much as it would be with the match, enticing you to stay with your employer for longer.

If you stay for another year, though, your total after Year 3 will continue to go up as your vesting is complete:

- Year 2 total + Year 3 principal ($4,000) = $12,734
- 6% gains on all of Year 3 ($12,734) = $764
- Total after Year 3 = $12,734 + $764 = $13,498

Now, after Year 3, you are officially vested. If you do decide to leave the company, 100% of the contributed money if yours to keep, forever. Of course, the longer you stay with the company the longer you can take advantage of their match and the longer your money can grow.

Money Goal!

It is very worthwhile to open a company-sponsored retirement plan, especially if it offers a match. And you should try to contribute at least as much as the company will match for the entire vesting period, at which time this "free" money becomes yours to keep.

Target-Date Retirement Funds

Target-date retirement funds are becoming increasingly popular in the United States. They can be purchased at almost any discount broker (like Vanguard, Fidelity, or Charles Schwab) and also have found a strong foothold in many of the company-sponsored retirement plans discussed in the preceding section.

Basically, the idea behind target-date retirement funds is wonderfully simple: you determine the approximate year in the future in which you want to retire, for example at age 60, and then you choose a target-date fund that is closest to that year. The fund automatically holds a certain percentage of stocks, cash equivalents, and other investments that is appropriate for your age and time horizon. As the years go by, the fund automatically rebalances and becomes incrementally more conservative so as to minimize any stock market losses close to your retirement and maintain as much principle as possible. These funds usually come in multiples of five-year increments: Target-date 2020, or Target-date 2035, for example.

Target-date funds can help eliminate the confusion that many employees and investors feel when they are faced with too many stock and mutual fund choices in the typical company-sponsored 401(k). This type of fund has become so popular that in 2006 the federal government deemed them an appropriate default option for a company's 401(k) if an employee does not choose any allocation when signing up for a retirement account.

Target-date funds are a great idea in theory. But the problem is that not all of these funds are created equal and not all investors are created equal. Consider the following two examples:

EXAMPLE #1:
Company A's 2040 target-date retirement fund holds 90% of its money in U.S. stocks, 5% in bonds, and 5% in Real Estate. Company B's 2040 target-date retirement fund holds only 60% of its money in U.S. stocks, 20% in bonds, and 20% in cash. Depending on which company you work for, you will have very different retirement funds and perhaps very different returns, even though the maturation of both is the same year. Thus, the "same" target-date funds of different companies can vary greatly.

EXAMPLE #2:
Diego and Adam are both thirty years old in 2010. Each wants to retire at age 50, in the year 2030. Both work for the same firm and invest all retirement money in the company-sponsored 2030 target-date fund. At the moment, this fund has 85% of its holdings in stocks and 15% in bonds, meaning that the fund will experience some volatility because of its significant stock percentage, but could see large long-term rewards. For Diego, being a bit of a risk-taker, this is the perfect asset allocation. The problem is that Adam, who is by nature more conservative, cannot stand to see the market fluctuate and is willing to accept less return in order to minimize risk. But he cannot do anything about it because this company's 2030 target-date retirement fund uses the same ratios for everyone.

From these examples you can see that target-date retirement funds offer the ease of one-stop shopping, but all are not created equal, nor can they be adjusted to suit individual tastes.

Watch Out!

Many employees are not given much information regarding the philosophy behind target-date funds and how they should invest their money in them.

Many people, therefore, simply assume that their money is invested wisely if they chose a target-date retirement fund, when in fact plans and individual tastes can vary widely. Again, the idea is great and very practical—a single fund with a single goal and a single time-horizon. But each investor should understand the fund's philosophy and individual components before considering it as an investment option.

One final drawback to this type of investment is that many people who invest in target-date retirement funds also invest money in other funds that hold stocks and bonds. In other words, a person invests in a target-date fund and also allocates other money to similar investment vehicles. This completely defeats the purpose of the target-date fund. If you put your money in a target-date retirement fund *and* other investments, there will be overlap and you can potentially skew your originally-desired portfolio allocation. This adds additional risk and should be avoided.

Better education for those who invest in this type of fund would help control the few problems that exist with target-date retirement funds. But in general, if you have the investment knowledge to choose your asset allocation by yourself then these funds are probably not for you. For many others, though, the ease and straightforwardness of target-date retirement funds are indeed a wonderful idea.

Action Plan

Saving and investing for your retirement is a necessity. Everyone knows that one day they will probably want to stop working and enjoy the life around them that may include kids, grandkids, vacations, golf, etc. A good thing is that investing for retirement uses basically the same knowledge as outlined in the "Investment" section, but applies it to a different type of account. As we discussed in this chapter, because few companies offer traditional pensions anymore, it is often up to you to fund your own golden years. And here is how:

- First, as always, make sure you are free from damaging credit card debt.

- Then, make sure that your emergency savings account is fully funded. If you do not have at least six months' worth of savings, continue to fund this account. Once this is done, you are ready to put your money to work for you.

- Check with the human resources department or business office where you work and if available, sign up for your company retirement plan, probably called a 401(k) or a 403(b) depending on the type of institution at which you work. As you are talking to someone in that office, confirm that there is a company match offered.

- Find out if the company offers a set "asset allocation" plan and choose the one that best fits your needs. Most likely, if you are reading this book you have time on your side and you should choose either a *moderate* allocation with a decent percentage of stocks or an *aggressive* allocation with a large percentage of stocks. Make sure that at least 5% of your paycheck (and perhaps even more than that) is diverted automatically every month into the retirement account and never stop, ever. If your company does offer a match, make sure that you contribute enough to take full advantage of it. If you can increase the percentage of money from your paycheck going toward your retirement to upwards of 10%, and still have enough to cover your monthly expenses, make sure to do so.

- Open a Roth IRA, if your income permits, at one of the major online brokerage firms (like Vanguard, Fidelity, or Charles Schwab). Fund this account fully if you can, contributing $5,000 every year. If you cannot write a check for the full amount in one shot, contribute to the IRA as you would a company-sponsored plan by having a set amount diverted from your checking account every month. Remember, though, that you also need to *invest* the money within an IRA and the impetus is on you. Look through the "Investment" chapter and find some low-cost quality index funds that you can buy and mature. If you have questions about your IRA, all firms that offer one give free customer support over the phone and online, so do not be afraid to ask.

- Never stop contributing to your retirement accounts as you work. EVER.

Chapter Seven:

Final Action Plan

Final Action Plan

Peole's finances are an integral part of their lives. You cannot escape having to pay bills, pay taxes, save for retirement, pay for college, get your car fixed, buy groceries, and a thousand other things that require money. Most people do not have enough money, unfortunately. And everyone wishes for more. By following the simple advice presented in this book, you can dramatically aid yourself in having a bright financial future. So here is our final Action Plan.

First, consider your goals. This involves knowing your Annual Income Requirement and then determining a final goal of having twenty-five times this amount saved and invested. This amount is how much you need to have in order to comfortably stop working (if you want to) and enjoy some of the more important aspects of life. Hinging upon that, though, are the following steps to follow

It is important to note that these steps will not (and most likely cannot) be achieved in a few months, or even a few years. It can take most of your adult life to acquire your AIR x 25 and be able to retire. But the more productively you follow the advice herein, the easier (and quicker) achieving this goal will ultimately be.

Please also note that you will most likely be doing some—or many—of these steps simultaneously. While they are listed in a logical order to begin your quest to financial independence, you must pay your bills on time (Step 2) while also saving for retirement (Step 5), for example. So read the following steps and follow them to the best of your ability.

1) Get rid of credit card debt (if you do not have any credit card debt, congratulate yourself and skip to the next step). But if you do have credit card debt, follow the advice in the "Debt" chapter regarding how to form a payment plan and erase damaging interest payments, while also employing some of the money-saving suggestions discussed in the "Savings" chapter. Only when you are free from credit card debt can you begin your own path to financial independence.

2) Pay all bills on time, including Paying Yourself First.

3) Find ways to save money (and avoid frivolous spending) whenever you can.

4) Make sure to fully fund an emergency savings account with at least six months' worth of living expenses.

5) Contribute to your company or employer retirement plan, such as a 401(k), if one is available. Sign up immediately and aim to contribute at least 5% of your paycheck to this account, and more if you can. Make sure to take advantage of a company match, if there is one, to get all of that "free" money.

6) Open a Roth IRA (if your income permits you) at a discount brokerage firm like Vanguard, Fidelity, Charles Schwab, or TD Ameritrade, if you are eligible based on your income. Fund it fully every year if you can to take advantage of its many tax breaks. Keep money in a Roth IRA invested in an index fund that tracks the S&P 500 or some other stock market index.

7) If you plan on purchasing a home in the future, make sure to have at least 20% of the home's purchase price set aside as a down payment. This sum should not interfere with your emergency savings. Also plan on paying as much as you can in mortgage payments each month to shorten the life of the mortgage and, ideally, pay it off sooner than its maturity date.

8) After completing all of the above steps, if you still have additional money coming in, buy yourself a cold one and pat yourself on the back. You are better off than 99% of the people living on this planet. Then open an investment account at the same brokerage firm that holds your IRA and put your additional money into it. Again, it is good to tie this money to an index fund because you guarantee the market's long-term results. But with this additional money, you also can have a bit more freedom to explore other investment options if you so desire because your other financial obligations are met. Talk to a Certified Financial Planner at the brokerage house and

see what investments are available. Then grab another cold one and enjoy your life. You earned it!

Congratulations on arriving at the end of your first course in personal finance. Implementing the strategies in this guidebook will greatly aid you in achieving your monetary goals. Remember, though, that everyone's financial situation is different. These chapters do not offer personalized advice, but instead offer a manual of useful, logical, and sound financial practices. If you follow them, though, you will be well on your way along the Pathway to Financial Independence.

Acknowledgements

First and foremost, I wish to thank my wonderful wife, Pauli. She has given me the time to work on this project for countless hours over the course of many months. What began as a simple favor for a friend grew into a much bigger project than anything I had originally planned, and my wife bore the brunt of the commitment on my part. And I might also mention that she would make a phenomenal professional editor!

I would also like to thank all those people—both friends and family—who read drafts of this book during its various stages of production. I owe you an enormous debt of gratitude. Perhaps the practices outlined herein can give you a bit of thanks by aiding you in reaching your financial dreams. If not, an autographed copy of this book is in the mail and you should be receiving it shortly.

Finally, I cannot complete this section without acknowledging a few people whom I have never met, nor whom have ever met me. Nevertheless, these authors and investors gave me the financial knowledge and interest through their work to make this project possible. I have read numerous books and articles by each one of these archetypal financial educators, and my ideas merely supplement what they have originally offered: Jeremy Siegel, William Bernstein, Robert Kiyosaki, John Templeton, Andrew Tobias, Charles Schwab, John Bogle, Benjamin Graham, Jason Zweig, and Warren Buffett.

Countless thanks to all.

Yours,
DFC

About the Author

Drew F. Catanese is an assiduous and devoted student of personal finance. He loves helping others understand how to manage their money, eagerly sharing his knowledge with those who want to learn. A Spanish teacher by trade, the author also loves traveling to new places and experiencing new cultures with his wife and daughter.

Endnotes

- *Forbes* magazine, March 10, 2005 article entitled "Why so many new billionaires?" by Luisa Kroll and Lea Goldman
- *Wall Street Journal* June 24, 2009 "The Wealth Report" by Robert Frank
- "Experian Marketing Insight Snapshot" (March 2009). Accessed from www.creditcards.com
- National Foundation for Credit Counseling, 2009 Financial Literacy Survey (April 2009) Accessed from www.creditcards.com
- Sallie Mae, "How Undergraduate Students Use Credit Cards," (April 2009) Accessed from www.creditcards.com
- Demos.org, "The Economic State of Young America" (May 2008) Accessed from www.creditcards.com
- "Generation Broke: Growth of Debt Among Young Americans"
- CreditCards.com survey (December 2008) www.creditcards.com
- U.S. Bureau of Economic Analysis "Personal Saving Rate" http://www.bea.gov/BRIEFRM/SAVING.HTM 1/5/2009
- *Money* magazine 6/2009 "The Money Shrink" Tyler Cowen
- Luke Setzer, "Saving for Greatness." http://solohq.org/Articles/Setzer/Saving_for_Greatness.shtml
- [12] Rate of return taken from Standard and Poor's website, http://www.standardandpoors.com.
- [13] Jeremy Siegel. *Stocks for the Long Run*. McGraw-Hill Companies; 2nd edition (March 1, 1998)
- [14] Rate of return taken from Standard and Poor's website, http://www.standardandpoors.com.
- [15] Dow Jones Industrial Average information taken from its website, http://www.djaverages.com.

LaVergne, TN USA
20 July 2010
190088LV00003B/20/P